THE RTW CLASS

Tony Beard and James Whiting

Capital Transport

Published by Capital Transport Publishing
www.capitaltransport.com

ISBN 978 1 85414 488 1

Printed by Parksons Graphics

Front cover photo: *Tony Belton*
Title page: *Vintage Images*
Above: *Alan B. Cross, The Bus Archive*
Opposite top left: *Ray Golds*
Opposite top right: *Michael Beamish*
Back cover left: *Vintage Images*
Back cover right: *Fred Ivey*

ACKNOWLEDGEMENTS
Laurie Akehurst, Ian Armstrong, John Bennett
at The Bus Archive, Lawrie Bowles, Jim Hawkins,
Chris Holland, George Jasieniecki, Mike Lloyd,
Malcolm Papes, Doug Rose, Ian Smith and the staff
of the TfL Corporate Archives were all very helpful
in the compilation of this book. Michael Eyre worked
on many of the black and white images to bring out
their best.

LONDON BUS ROUTES
It is not practical to give full RTW route details
in most cases but these are easily to be found on
the enthusiasts' website Londonbuses.co.uk or by
reference to Mike Harris's excellent series of historical
bus maps.

VEHICLE HISTORIES
For full details of allocations, body and chassis
numbers and overhaul dates, we very much recommend
the publication *London Transport Vehicle Histories:
RTW Class* by Lawrie Bowles, John A S Hambley and
Alan Bond (A Transport Interest Publication, 2000)

Moves to Wider Buses

The last air raids of the London Blitz had yet to occur when, on 1st May 1941, Vernon Robertson, Engineer in Chief of the London Passenger Transport Board, penned a report entitled 'Bus Rolling Stock Replacements After the War'. In this he anticipated that a programme of new buses could commence in 1943, assuming the war was over by then. At the time, London Transport owned 6,306 petrol and oil public service vehicles, many of which were nearing the end of their useful lives, then given as twelve years for a double-deck bus, and on that basis around 1,000 would soon fall due for replacement. Robertson also recorded that, as the Board was legally restricted to the production of 527 bodies per annum from its works, the balance would have to be purchased locally at prices above the Board's manufacturing costs.

Robertson's report provoked a myriad of responses from his fellow officers regarding the design of the post war fleet and from these the requirement for five basic types of vehicles emerged, headed by a general purpose double-deck bus for either coach or bus operation according to the body fitted for which the RT was thought ideally suited. The RT was the product of four years research by the Board's Technical Department at Chiswick and no departure from the construction of the body was thought necessary, which after two years in service had provided very encouraging results.

The objective regarding dimensions was to secure sanctions for an overall length of 30ft (the maximum then permitted was 26ft) and a width of 8ft in place of the 7ft 6ins currently enforced. The change in overall width was of great interest to the Board in view of the greater latitude it would allow for gangways and elbow room. There was a call for a maximum seating capacity of 60 but in consideration of this suggestion came a comment that this number was only required during one hour each in mornings and evenings during which each bus could only achieve one return journey. It was therefore suggested that any additional capacity beyond the current average of 56 could be provided by standing room achieved by wider gangways.

From the interested officers' contributions, recommendations for the double-deck post war fleet were itemised as follows:

(a) The basic life of all new vehicles should be 12 years.
(b) The chassis should be the RT for the first six post-war years of replacement with such modifications to its specification arising between 1942 and the end of the war and that any further modifications should be developed and applied as soon as possible.
(c) The basic type of body should be the RT as previously discussed.
(d) That every step should be taken to formulate decisions regarding weight, length and width restrictions.
(e) That chassis types adopted, other than AEC, should be, as far as possible, to the Board's specification and drawings.

By the time that a plan for 8ft buses was first raised, the Board had already gained experience in the operation of vehicles of this dimension. During early 1941, the Board was informed that there was a possibility of securing 25 trolleybuses that were in the process of being manufactured for service in Durban, South Africa; U-boat activity in the Atlantic prevented their departure. The Ministry of War Transport and the Metropolitan Police subsequently gave approval to the operation of the vehicles, each of which weighed a ton more than the London standard trolleybus and, having been constructed using a standard width chassis, the front wheel spacing was extended using studs. Once adapted for work in London, the vehicles, together with a further eighteen that should have been shipped to Johannesburg, were allocated to Ilford Depot from which the local routes were thought ideal due to the absence of any over-bridges, the vehicles being higher than normal.

In early 1943 a joint report was produced on behalf of the road transport institutions regarding the proposed revision of regulations affecting public service vehicles. Within the report, four amendments to the existing regulations were sought, three were dimensional covering length, width and height while the fourth sought an increase in the maximum permissible axle load by requesting an increase for public service vehicles to 9½ tons with no restriction placed on the maximum laden vehicle weight. The second amendment pursued was for the maximum overall width to be increased to 8ft as this dimension was permitted in most countries with the notable exception of Great Britain. The current width of 7ft 6ins was thought inadequate for transverse seating, particularly in winter months when overcoats were worn. Conductors were also unable to collect fares efficiently, especially when standing passengers were carried.

And there the issue rested, especially as Roberton's hypothesis of the war concluding by the end of 1943 proved extremely inaccurate and the Board was forced to continue operating a fleet consisting of many buses that were long past their date of withdrawal and relying on supplies of austerity vehicles.

No information is available about the trial running of the two 8ft wide mock-up vehicles along proposed routes, the object of the experiment being to obtain approval of the service operation of the 8ft bus. After the completion of tests, chassis 0961023, on which this mock-up body is mounted, became RT 1117. This bus entered service from Muswell Hill garage in February 1949, while 0961037 became RT 2436, this vehicle entering service from Old Kent Road garage the following December.
British Transport Films

At a Joint Consultative Committee Meeting (JCC) of AEC and the LPTB in late December 1944, word had been received from the Ministry of War Transport rejecting any proposed alterations to vehicle dimensions. A recommendation was therefore made for the Board to order from AEC 500 RT chassis for delivery commencing December 1945, building up to the rate of ten per week as rapidly as possible. The chassis were to be constructed to a revised specification and some testing lay ahead with AEC being given access to two RT chassis of early wartime manufacture for modification to the post-war layout. These were RT 52, to which AEC undertook some alterations between June 1944 and March 1945, and later RT 19. The latter became known as the 3RT prototype, with it having been subjected to a more thorough modification programme.

On 2nd February 1946, the Board and AEC received notification at one of their meetings that the Ministry of Transport had sanctioned the use of 8ft wide buses on certain routes. In consequence its members thought it desirable for a decision to be reached in respect of the post war RT programme, with discussions continuing throughout the early months of that year.

Schemes for the introduction of a chassis frame and axles of increased width to which could be fitted larger wheels and tyres were put forward by AEC for examination by the Board. In exchange, the Board supplied information to AEC relative to the estimated increase in weight of an 8ft wide body with a rider that a turning circle of 56ft was required.

By March the Board had submitted schemes demonstrating the utilisation of the increased width allowance and the stability of such vehicles, but there was some speculation that the new width would worsen the position for attaining the

required tilting angle of 28 degrees. The Board took responsibility for all tilting tests and use was made of RT 19, whose chassis had received the body from RT 1 soon after its return from AEC on 27th November 1945.

When tilt testing took place, the axles of RT 19's chassis had been extended to simulate conditions applicable to an 8ft wide vehicle; the overall width across the front tyres was 7ft 11 ins, while that across the rear tyres was 7ft 9¼ ins. The chassis achieved a tilting angle of 27 degrees and 28 degrees following the fitting of different wheels. In the outcome, RT 19 was tilted with the body and chassis frame rigidly attached to the axles and a titling angle of 30 degrees for the whole vehicle was achieved. A recommendation was also made for the proposed chassis frame of 8ft vehicles to be increased in width to enable a greater distance between springs thereby achieving greater vehicle stability.

By June 1946, AEC made it clear that should an increased width between the chassis frame members be required, production could not commence until 1948. If, however, the standard chassis frame width with modifications to wheels, axles and some cab fittings was acceptable, supplies could commence earlier; the Board then still favoured a wider chassis.

It was decided that the frame width should be increased to the maximum allowable figure and drawings were to be submitted indicating the extent of alterations involved. Agreement was also reached regarding the first chassis which, when produced, would be fitted with a prototype body for testing before AEC was committed to production.

During May 1946, the Board took delivery of two RT chassis at Chiswick for use in an experiment to ascertain the possibility of operating 8ft wide buses on streets in central London. The wheel separation was subsequently extended by the use of specially fabricated tubes and skeletal bodies were fitted, there being some RT style influence in their construction.

The draft specification for the second order for 500 RT chassis was reviewed by the JCC and approved for distribution in mid-July and during discussion the question was raised of whether these would be 7ft 6ins in width. It was agreed that the original stipulation should be followed unless an alteration to vehicle width was decided by higher authority, but by the next meeting it was agreed that the specification would apply to 250 7ft 6ins wide chassis and arrangements made for 250 further sets of components to be produced that were common to both widths.

Although the specifications applied to chassis of AEC manufacture, the Board had also considered purchasing a supply from Leyland Motors Ltd and there was now a need to create some uniformity if two suppliers were to be involved, the first issue covering the position of the controls and steering column. AEC planned to move these 3ins towards the offside of the chassis built to support an 8ft body while Leyland had recommended the controls should be moved 2ins. Clearly a compromise was needed and it was agreed that the Board should endeavour to persuade Leyland and AEC to settle on 2½ ins. AEC agreed to comply with a measurement suitable to Leyland thereby maintaining a standardisation of bodies, the design of which could now be finalised.

On 1 January 1947, JCC members convened and were informed that the order for the first 500 8ft wide vehicles had been placed with Leyland, the Board having finalised the roof and platform heights of the body which should remain standard and interchangeable on Leyland and AEC chassis.

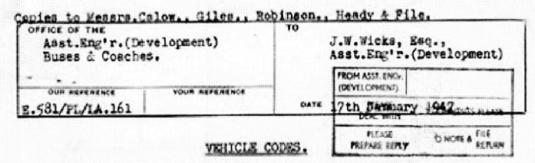

OFFICE OF THE	TO
Asst.Eng'r.(Development) Buses & Coaches.	J.W.Wicks, Esq., Asst.Eng'r.(Development)

OUR REFERENCE	YOUR REFERENCE		FROM ASST. ENG. (DEVELOPMENT)
E.581/PL/IA.161		DATE	17th January 1947

VEHICLE CODES.

| PLEASE PREPARE REPLY | NOTE & RETURN | FILE |

I attach hereto proposed Vehicles Codes for the RT range of chassis and bodies for both 7'-6" and 8'-0" design.

You will note that I propose using the letter "RT" for Leylands although this brand of chassis has always been identified as "STD".

As I am anxious to establish the appropriate codes for D.O. and Specification purposes, I shall be glad if you will give me direction as soon as possible.

In establishing the code please bear in mind the complications which will result if you decide to adhere to "STD" for Leylands, as the RT3/1 bodies are interchangeable for the first time in the Board's history with the A.E.C. chassis and you will get the following awkward vehicle code:

Chassis Code.	Body Code.	Vehicle Code.
5 STD	RT3/1	5 STD.RT3/1

Pursuing the above vehicle code the bonnet number will be STD..... which indicates the brand of chassis manufacture for Licencing and Publicity purposes, but to my mind, gives the wrong impression as the main bulk of the vehicle is in fact "RT" design.

Might I suggest, as an alternative, that these new Leyland chassis be identified by the letter "L" denoting Leyland which is comparable with the already established "D" for Daimler, "B" for Bristol and "G" for Guy.

Thus the code would become as follows, and the RT body identity would not disappear.

Chassis Code.	Body Code.	Vehicle Code.
2L	RT3/1	2LRT3/1

Pursuing the above, the bonnet number will be LRT....

CHIEF DRAUGHTSMAN.

The 1500 Leyland chassis were originally to be coded 5STD, though there was no intention to number the finished buses in the STD series. A memo dated 17th January 1947 raised the issue of body codes not agreeing with chassis codes if the STD code was used for the latter as it had been up to now for the Leyland PD Type. It was suggested that the buses be classified LRT (for Leyland RT), a code which, had it been adopted, may have led to the RTW being classified as WRT. Handwritten notes in the margin of the copy seen show other possibilties for the Leylands, i.e. RL, RLW or RTW. *The Bus Archive*

By February details of the completed negotiations with Leyland were made available. Leyland had designed the chassis for the purpose adapting their own PD2/3 to meet the Board's specific requirements which included an AEC transmission. In consequence the Board was still in the process of designing the 8ft body based on the chassis dimensions which now reflected a departure from the initial proposals that AEC had submitted. The Board asked AEC to give consideration to standardising its main chassis dimensions for the future but George Rackham, AEC's Chief Engineer responded by recording that he did not currently find it opportune to take such action, and requested that the issue should be deferred until January 1948 when the Leyland design was more advanced. He also stated that AEC's original agreement to supply 8ft units within three months of instructions from the Board was now impracticable.

And there AEC's immediate involvement ceased in the construction of chassis for the new 8ft wide for London Transport buses. As we know, nothing more was to come of it.

Although by the time RTL 1 was delivered in November 1948, it had clearly been decided against using a common series of fleet numbers for all of the Leylands, the first use of the code RTW found in official documents was in March 1949, the month RTW 1 arrived at Chiswick. Prior to then, documents refer only to the '8ft wide Leyland'. It cannot be assumed that it had been intended at first to use RTL for both widths of Leyland even if all of the buses were contained within one number block. Differentiation would have been needed, not least at garage level where the 8-footers would need to be restricted to particular routes.

Negotiations with Leyland

On 19 June 1947, a quotation was received from Leyland for the supply of 500 bodies built to the Board's special design which amounted to £2,750 each, later revised to £2,545.

A meeting was convened, chaired by Henry Spurrier, Leyland's Managing Director; the Board was represented by A B B Valentine (Chief Supplies Officer), A A M Durrant Chief Mechanical Engineer (Buses and Coaches) and E Ottaway (Technical Officer Buses and Coaches). In acknowledging Leyland's quote, Valentine stated that this was considerably in excess of the figure compiled by the Board's Estimating Department, of £1,975, and consequently he stated that he would be required to provide the Board with a very good explanation to account for the difference before its members were likely to accept it. The maximum estimated price for a standard 7ft 6ins wide body was £1,730.

Spurrier intimated that his company was quite prepared to review the compilation of the figure quoted, it having been based upon the requirement for additional labour and material over and above the standard body.

During the debate that followed a reduction was sought as the development cost of the body had already been borne by the Board. Spurrier suggested that if the order were increased to 1,000, the cost would be £2,480 each for 500 and a reduction of £100 on the balance resulting in £2,380 for the second 500 provided the orders ran concurrently. In making this offer, Leyland would need to give consideration to the delivery programme and requested a response by April 1948, which Durrant thought reasonable knowing that the Board was not in a position to make a quick decision. The earliest delivery for the commencement of deliveries of 500 complete vehicles was given as late August 1948.

The meeting concluded with a brief discussion regarding future double-deck bus development and Spurrier stated that Leyland had been working on modified designs for some time with the object of eliminating timber and reducing the weight of bodies by the combined use of aluminium extrusions with pressed steelwork. The company had also given some thought to chassisless construction but it was felt that the scope in that direction was limited while a rear entrance and exit remained in use. No mention was made of revised dimensions by either party despite the meeting having discussed the construction of London's first 8ft wide motor buses.

By November 1947, the Board had provisionally accepted Leyland's revised quotation of £2,480 for each body but were hopeful of further reductions which could see this reduced to £2,425. It was this figure that was included in a list comparing bus body prices, the number to which each refers appears in parenthesis:

Park Royal £2,464 (500), Leyland £2,425 (500), Saunders £2,500 (250), Craven £2,520 (120) and Metropolitan-Cammell-Weymann £2,485 (1,000). The issue of the body price appears to have been settled in January 1948 when the price was agreed at £2,480 each. The bodies were to be Leyland's own specification employing a metal-framed construction but suitably styled to harmonise with the Executive's post-war fleet.

The Board supplied Leyland with its specification for 500 56-seat 8ft-wide bodies on 15 August 1947; they were to be classified RT6.

Specifications issued to Weymann and Park Royal for their RT bodies were far more extensive, the plans having been drawn at Chiswick, but in this case, the structure was of Leyland design yet the bodies were required to conform to LT's principles in respect of interchangeability.

Although Leyland's structural principles would form the basis of the body, the Board required its contours to be as close as possible to those of RT3/1 which could then be applied to suit the wider body by the insertion of 3inches either side of the longitudinal centre line, although the framing for the cab floor and the rear end of the upper saloon required special treatment.

The nearside front wing of the RT was a complete departure from that applied to earlier double deck vehicles. Initially fitted to the 10T10 Green Line coaches and trialled on two STL vehicles, this patented design was specified but was to be modified to suit the 8ft body. The roof framework was to conform as far as possible to the Board's profile

The interiors of the saloons were to be trimmed to match those of the RT type. The headroom inside the lower saloon was given as 5ft 10¾ ins, while that for the upper saloon was 5ft 8½ ins.

The seat frames fitted inside the saloons would have their distance from the sides increased by one inch, with a spacer filling the gap. This enabled the seats for 7ft 6in vehicles and 8ft vehicles to be identical and capable of accepting standard cushions and squabs although the Board's specification suggests that these would only be interchangeable with other 8ft vehicles.

The principal measurements were length: 25ft 11³/₈ins, width: 7ft 10ins (over structure), 7ft 11 ins, (overall); unladen height 14ft 4ins ± ³/₈ins.

There was little difference between the chassis for the RTL and RTW, the profile of each being designed to match London Transport's specification. To gain extra width a standard rear axle was used with extended hubs. However, the wider RTW front axle was made from two sections joined off-centre, that on the RTL was was cast as a single unit.

London's first 8ft wide motor bus, RTW 1 is on the tilt test in Leyland's works in February 1949. The manufacturer called it the gravity test and in this view the bus has reached the 40 degree tilt aimed for to meet London Transport's requirements. Fleet name and destination blind masking are in place, so the bus looks ready for delivery to Chiswick works. Fleet number is missing, suggesting that the code RTW may not have been decided on by this late stage. *BCVM*

Throughout production Leyland used LT's classification 6RT for identification of the chassis as it differed considerably from the Titan PD2/3 with which it has often but incorrectly been associated. All major components apart from the engine and steering were to LT specification. The engine was a relatively new 0.600 9.8 litre diesel with an output of 125 bhp at 1800 rpm but derated, as those fitted to the RT type, to 115 bhp which provided for a longer life in service. It fitted quite closely into the engine compartment and in consequence required a degree of modification.

The Board's Special Expenditure Requisition (SER) No 15/2257 dated 3 December 1947 was issued for 1,000 RTL chassis at £1,423 each, 500 RTW chassis at £1,433 each and 500 RTW bodies at £2,480 each, each complete RTW costing £3,913. However, the SER was later revised, due to a rise and fall clause included in the contract, the cost of the whole class becoming £2,252,104 with the cost of each vehicle increasing to £4,504.

First Allocations

The Board's Bus Allocation Advisory Committee first convened on 29th November 1946, under the chairmanship of J B Burnell Operating Manager (Central Road Services), its remit being to manage the future introduction of the standardised fleet. As such the Committee continued in this capacity after the formation of the London Transport Executive on 1 January 1948.

The first issue recorded was the bottleneck being experienced in the supply of new buses, the number of new double deck RT buses to be delivered by the end of 1946 having been reduced from 110 to nil. Estimates for the ensuing years of 910 in 1947 and 1,910 in 1948 fell to 311 and 1,208.

A further scaling down was anticipated as the figures were based on calculations made by the body builders, estimated chassis deliveries being far in excess of body completion. However, the Board did not accept this position and officers were making every effort to improve upon deliveries and negotiations were in hand for the supply of 1,500 vehicles over and above the estimated figures. Nevertheless, RTW deliveries were not expected to commence until March 1948 and the full effect not appreciated until the following year.

In addition, the introduction of 8ft wide buses was now being discussed with the Regional Transport Commissioner who remained unconvinced that they should be permitted on routes passing through the City and West End.

Arrangements were made for routes and garages to be surveyed using the two specially constructed vehicles in order that a definite allocation could be made for the wider vehicles. However, since it was proving impossible to assess accurately the effects of the increased width operation in the City and West End with just two vehicles, it was agreed to introduce the 8ft wide vehicles on a complete route basis. They would be transferred from the outer areas and if not found satisfactory could be returned to their original routes. By this means the possibility of a considerable number of 8ft wide buses being found unsuitable would be avoided although the committee members agreed that delay in the large scale introduction of the wider vehicles would occur.

During discussions relating to the Country Area, there emerged some understanding that testing might commence in 1947. While Green Line services would automatically follow the decision relating to central London certain routes that avoided this area could be equipped with 8ft wide coaches.

Meetings of the Bus Allocation Advisory Committee were sporadic throughout the remaining months of the LPTB, its members convening only three times during 1947, but with just 182 RTs delivered throughout that year, there was little to be achieved. April 1948 saw the first meeting of the committee under the London Transport Executive during which mention was made of the 8ft wide vehicles, there being an indication that deliveries might commence at the end of the year. The vehicles would be allocated to garages in the outer Central Area for working on routes agreed with the Ministry of Transport and Metropolitan Police following a series of practical tests using the two 'mock-up' vehicles. The routes approved would account for 470 of the type, the remaining 30 being used as spare vehicles; in a number of situations standard RTs would be displaced.

By August, information was received regarding the failure to secure authority for the operation of 8ft wide buses in the Country Area and the committee also thought it inadvisable to operate the vehicles over tram routes. It was also decided that Tottenham, Seven Kings and Bromley garages should be removed from the allocation of the second batch of RTs in view of the early allocation of 8ft wide buses to work on approved routes.

The Committee endorsed the intention to conduct a large scale test using the vehicles on inner London routes which would be involve all authorities concerned but further problems lay ahead when it was realised that structural alterations would be necessary at some garages designated to receive the wider buses which were higher than standard and would make contact with roofs and entrances; fuelling islands would also require alteration. In consequence, difficulties were experienced in locating sufficient routes to absorb the whole of the order. Some routes were satisfactory but were mainly on the outskirts and separated from one another so that the allocation tended to be for a few buses at a large number of garages. Other routes needed minor or major road alterations the completion of which could not be guaranteed, while a number of routes presented special problems that caused the Licensing Authority to withhold approval pending substantial experience of wider bus working. There were additional difficulties in route allocation arising from the practice whereby buses on routes now approved could conceivably be allocated to work on routes not approved and the utmost care was requested to avoid loss of bus availability due to the restrictions imposed on the wider vehicles.

Opposite: The original typed document showing the initial plans for the allocation of the 500 RTWs. 'Routes Completed' refers to routes that had been surveyed and approved for 8ft wide buses.

ALLOCATION OF 500 8' WIDE RT TYPE BUSES (CENTRAL AREA)
(exclusive of engineering spares)

GARAGES (in suggested order of priority)	8' WIDE BUSES ≠ (see notes)	ROUTES APPROVED AND BUSES ALLOCATED THERETO												7'6" WIDE BUSES ∮ (see notes)	REMARKS
		Route	Buses	Present type	Route	Buses	Present type	Route	Buses	Present type	Route	Buses	Present type		
TOTTENHAM	22	41	32	LT										-	
ALPERTON	25	187	25	ST										-	
SHEPHERDS BUSH	22	105	22	LT										-	) Completion of
HANWELL	43	92	17	B	105	26	LT & STL							-	) Route 105.
WEST GREEN	15	144	10	LT	144A	5	LT							37	) Completion of
ENFIELD	8	144A	8	G										-	) Routes 144 and
LEYTON	14	144	14	RT ∮										77	) 144A.
PALMERS GREEN	26	112	26	STL										-	
PUTNEY BRIDGE	10	85	10	STL										-	
HARROW WEALD	42	140	17	STL	158	25	STL							-	) Completion of
EDGWARE	37	140	16	STL	142	21	STL							-	) Route 140.
UPTON PARK	20	129	6	RT ∮	145	14	LT							48	) Completion of
BARKING	19	23B	5	G	23C	9	LT	145	5	LT				32	) Route 145.
SEVEN KINGS	49	86	5	LT	139	14	LT	149	4	RT ∮	148	26	LT & ST	26	) Completion of
HORNCHURCH	4	86	4	G										-	) Route 86.
BROMLEY	25	119	12	STL	126	8	STL	138	5	STL				41	
LOUGHTON	16	20	16	STD										-	
TURNHAM GREEN	34	91	34	RT ∮										36	
UXBRIDGE	3	225	3	ST (7'6" RT allocation outstanding) ∮										9	
	* 444	exclusive of engineering spares													

ROUTES COMPLETED: 20, 23B/C, 41, 85, 86, 91, 92, 105, 112, 119, 126, 129, 138, 139, 140, 142, 144, 144A, 145, 147, 148, 158, 187 and 225.

NOTES: ≠ Allocation based on 1948 schedules for approved routes.

∮ 7'6" wide RT's already allocated to these garages as previously agreed.

∮ 7'6" wide RT's already on these routes will be re-allocated.

* In certain cases the present schedules provide for buses on the approved routes also to operate on certain other routes NOT APPROVED for 8' wide operation; in consequence certain adjustments to these figures will be necessary.

18th August, 1948.
C/SS
(40)

By March 1949, the 8ft-wide vehicles had received the code letters RTW, the last letter indicating 'wide' and the Allocation Committee received notice that the first of the type would soon be available for training. It had now become necessary for an agreement to be reached regarding the priority of allocation for which a provisional list had already been prepared and distributed. This gave Tottenham garage first priority (route 41 with an allocation of 32 buses) followed by Alperton (route 187 with 25 buses).

RTW 1 arrived at Chiswick on 1 March 1949 and remained the sole representative of the class for ten weeks. Deliveries were slower than anticipated, 87 having been expected up to August but only 54 had been delivered. However, a steady output continued and the weekly total increased from two and three in the early period to eight and nine thereafter, a total of 213 being on the Executive's books by the end of the year, which equated with the number programmed.

RTW 1 entered service from Tottenham garage on route 41 in May 1949, but moved to Alperton garage in August. It was the first of 37 RTWs allocated to the 41 to replace 20-year-old LT double deckers built for the LGOC, some with open staircases. The smart new buses were way ahead in design alongside these vintage vehicles, whose life had been prolonged by the war. RTWs 2 and 3 also started work that month, to be followed by RTWs 4–14 and 16 in June, 15 and 17–27 in July and 28–37 in August.

On 13th April 1949 route 41 at Tottenham garage had the honour of being the first to receive RTWs and therefore the first 8ft wide motor buses in London. Its Monday to Saturday peak hour extension to Ilford took it into the territory of London's first 8ft wide trolleybuses, the vehicles diverted from South African orders owing to the war. The new RTWs (1–37) would have been a big contrast to the aged LT types, around 20 years old at the time. The two types operated side by side on the route for over six months while the new buses were gradually placed into service. *C. Carter*

At the time RTWs were introduced, route 187 ran between South Harrow Station and Hampstead Heath. RTWs were introduced on 3rd September 1949 and RTW 62 is seen at Kensal Rise in this view taken soon after the route was converted with a scheduled allocation of 25. The new buses took over from STs at Alperton that had been joined on Saturdays by STLs from Willesden. On Sundays the route had been in the hands of Alperton's utility G type buses, so regular users of the route had been accustomed to some wide-ranging variety. *C. Carter*

Route 187 from Alperton garage was the next route to receive the new buses, the first arriving in August. This conversion, from ST type, was completed the following month. This was followed by the 105 (Shepherd's Bush and Hanwell – shortly to be renamed Southall) between September and October. October then saw Leyton's route 144 receive the new buses and the 144A from Enfield followed in November, when West Green garage, which also operated a share of both routes, started to get RTWs as well.

Route 112 (Palmers Green) followed the same month, a conversion completed in December, when route 85 (Putney Bridge) began and completed its conversion. The last garages to receive RTWs in 1949 were Harrow Weald and Edgware, which were allocated them for routes 140, 142 and 158 in a changeover from STLs completed in the first month of 1950. Route 142 had some STDs on Sundays from Hendon and these remained to run alongside RTWs until May 1952.

After the 187, RTWs began to appear on route 105 (Shepherd's Bush Garage to Southall Brent Road), meeting RTWs on the 187 at Hanger Lane. The route was shared between Shepherd's Bush garage and Hanwell garage (renamed Southall the following October) with a scheduled allocation of 26 buses from each. RTW 81 was photographed at Greenford. *Alan B. Cross, The Bus Archive*

The 144 followed with RTWs at Leyton garage from October. Enfield garage's 144A received them in November alongside the completion of Leyton's allocation to the route and their introduction on West Green's share of both routes. This view shows RTW 123 just north of Waterworks Corner, Woodford. *Roy Vincent*

The 112 was the third RTW route to serve Hanger Lane, beginning in November and completing in December. The route had a summer Sunday extension to Hampton Court, which was worked by RTWs in summer 1951 and, possibly, at least part of summer 1950. Here, RTW 154 is seen outside Palmers Green garage in March 1950. *Alan B. Cross, The Bus Archive*

Route 85 was the first RTW route to serve areas south of the Thames on a regular basis. Except during the 1950 width trials and while trams were still running, as they were in many south and south east parts of London, RTWs were not introduced on routes that ran alongside them in case the clearance was too tight. The 85 started to receive RTWs at Putney Bridge garage on 3rd May 1950 and had a scheduled allocation of ten of the type seven days a week, joined by four 2RT2s on Saturdays when more buses were needed. RTW 426 is seen at Kingston in 1951. *Simon Butler*

Harrow Weald was next to receive RTWs, doing so from December 1949 for its route 158, which at that time ran between Watford Junction and Ruislip. Eight of the buses were second hand, being transferred from Tottenham and it had received enough for its allocation by the beginning of February, when the 140 immediately followed. Also in February, Edgware started to get an allocation of RTWs for its share of this route, then going on to get further RTWs for use on its 142. On Sundays for a short time, Edgware's RTWs ran on this alongside pre-war STDs from Hendon. *J.H. Aston*

In January Upton Park got 19 RTWs for routes 129 and 145. It shared the latter route with Barking, which started to get RTWs in March 1950. At the end of that month, and during the deliveries of the type to Barking, RTWs began to arrive in the livery that omitted the cream relief around the upper deck windows. The first was RTW 286. Once the 145 allocation was completed the new buses continued to arrive at Barking garage for use on special works services 23B (Barking to Becontree, Mon-Sat peaks only), 23C (Creekmouth Power Station to Barking daily; extended to Becontree Mon- Fri peaks only) and 148 (Leytonstone to Dagenham). *Alan B. Cross, The Bus Archive, and C. Carter*

By 1st January 1950 the highest numbered RTW in service was RTW 204. The type was destined to start appearing on central London routes later that year, but before then more introductions on suburban services would occur.

By 3rd April 1950, questions were being raised regarding the allocation to Hornchurch and Seven Kings garages in view of neither having received any RTWs. The officer responsible stated that the original allocation list from August 1948 showed these garages to be in the bottom third of the nineteen garages approved. He then suggested that Hornchurch should not receive the four RTWs as originally intended and that Seven Kings should only receive 40 instead of 49. His purpose was twofold: (a) to avoid the introduction of RTWs on route 86 which was worked jointly with route 86A, the latter not being approved for the wider buses and (b) to avoid the allocation of so small a number of RTWs into a garage that had a large fleet of one type of double decker.

Also under debate were the disadvantages of sending 3 RTWs to Uxbridge and 34 to Turnham Green, the latter having a new fleet of RTLs and a number of RTs that were the subjects of experiments due to the proximity of the garage to Chiswick Works. It was decided not to send RTWs to these two garages or Hornchurch.

A further situation arose regarding route 144B at Enfield garage. From a report received it was noted that route 144B was the only part of the 144 group not approved for wide bodied vehicle operation and the working of RTWs, subsequently on a Sunday eight RTWs were dormant. On Saturdays and Sundays there were insufficient RTLs and the only available alternative was to use Guy buses. To partly alleviate the problem Enfield would receive RTLs from Tottenham garage at weekends.

Barking garage's share of the 148 was a small one and its partner on the route, Seven Kings followed with the buses for its allocation and also the 139 and 145, which were completed by the end of June, by which time the central London width trials with the type had taken place. RTW 48 is seen at Dagenham New Road and RTW 353 at Gants Hill, outside the Valentines public house. *Allen T. Smith, The Bus Archive*

After Harrow Weald's 140 and 158 had been dealt with, the next routes to receive them were six from east London garages Barking, Upton Park and Seven Kings, these being works services 23B and 23C and the 129, 139, 145 and 148. The RTWs on the 23B were introduced alongside RTLs and utility Gs interworked from other services. These conversions took place between January and June 1950 and it was during these conversions that the first of the famous width trials occurred on potentially suitable central London routes. These are covered in the next chapter and were to lead to most of the suburban services on which the type had started its life losing their RTWs.

In June it was Bromley garage's turn to receive RTWs. They were used on routes 119, 126 and 138, on which they ran until their buses were moved to central London routes. Introduction of the buses on purely suburban services was by now coming to an end, with just the 92 and 92A from Southall garage following in August. The last suburban conversion, one month after RTWs began to move to central London on a permanent basis, was Harrow Weald's 114 in October.

At an Informal Road Services meeting held on 9th August 1950, those present were informed that part of a hangar at Langley Airfield, east of Slough, had been rented for the sole purpose of fitting cab heaters to RT family vehicles. This work was carried out at Langley from January 1951 onwards, though. RTW 1 and RTW 2 had cab heaters fitted during their initial overhauls in November 1951 and January 1952. The class did not last long enough in service to have saloon heaters fitted. The same was the case with the RTL class, which followed their wider brothers into London Transport's history books two and a half years after the RTWs.

The first outer south-east London garage to receive RTWs was Bromley, where routes 119, 126 and 138 were converted in June and early July. In fact, it was not only the first garage in this part of London to receive them, it was the only one ever to. Outer south London was not an area to see many RTWs until later years when Brixton garage had a sizeable allocation. RTW 381 is seen at Bromley North. *Roy Marshall*

Southall was no stranger to RTWs and received more in August, this time for routes 92 and 92A. RTW 113, one of the buses allocated to the garage for the 105 the previous October is seen at the Wembley Empire Pool terminus next to B 2 in April 1950. Southall used its RTWs on the 92 and 92A at weekends, nominally alongside STLs, prior to full conversion.
Alan B. Cross, The Bus Archive

Harrow Weald likewise already had RTWs, for routes 140 and 158, and in October the 114 was converted as the last purely suburban route to receive them. Here they replaced STLs and SRTs. RTW 32 is seen on a wet day in Harrow Weald being overtaken by an STL demoted to a staff bus towards the end of its days.
Alan B. Cross, The Bus Archive

In addition to Alperton using spare RTWs at weekends on routes 92 and 92A, it also used them on route 83, on which RTW 52 is seen. Unlike the 92/A, the 83 did not otherwise receive a scheduled allocation of the buses.
Alan B. Cross, The Bus Archive

Upton Park used spare RTWs from routes 129 and 145 on route 86 on Saturdays and Seven Kings added a Sunday allocation of them from early 1951 until it lost its RTWs later that year. RTW 322 is seen in Romford. The 86 reached the farthest from central London of any scheduled RTW working at Brentwood. The 47 came second in reaching the farthest south-east with RTWs to Farnborough, the 158 reached Watford Junction in the north-west and the 14A RTWs in 1950 reached Hampton Court in the south-west. *Alan B. Cross, The Bus Archive*

Seven Kings also used RTWs on route 150 on Saturdays and Sundays, which first appear in the schedules book for October 1950 (though they probably started before then). RTW 327 is seen at Ilford. *Alan B. Cross, The Bus Archive*

The 102 had a longer history with RTWs but it began with a Saturday only operation from Tottenham where spare vehicles from the weekend 41 allocation were used. *Alan B. Cross, The Bus Archive*

Palmers Green's route 112 RTWs supplied five for use on a brief summer Sunday only operation on route 29 in 1950. The buses worked shorts between Turnpike Lane and Cockfosters (for Trent Park). RTW 158 is seen at Palmers Green. *Alan B. Cross, The Bus Archive*

The Width Trials

Four years were to elapse between the original suggestion in 1946 for 8ft wide vehicles to be evaluated on a route that served the City and West End and the actual testing.

With nearly half of the order of 500 RTWs now delivered, J B Burnell reported to an informal Road Services meeting of the Executive held on 15th February 1950, that he understood the police would only require a limited test on these vehicles in central London instead of the concentration of the whole RTW fleet envisaged in earlier deliberations. As a result, Durrant was requested to report upon the length of time required for the production of additional wider vehicles on the assumption that no application would be made for the tests before September 1950. Durrant responded on 1st March 1950 stating that a changeover to the wider vehicles by Park Royal Vehicles and Weymann would necessitate the employment of additional staff and considerable preliminary design work at the conclusion of which a period of 18 months would elapse before the delivery of the first vehicle. In consequence of the trials proving successful, if conducted and approved by the end of 1950, further wider vehicles would not begin to enter the fleet until the first half of 1952 when the current cycle of bus replacements was nearing completion.

On account of a possible change in vehicle design, it was agreed that Durrant should make contact with the Assistant Commissioner, H Dalton, of the Metropolitan Police, suggesting that steps might now be taken to test 8ft wide buses in central London. Durrant wasted no time and in his letter on 2nd March he reminded Dalton of the conference held in 1946 when a number of routes on the periphery of the Central Area were approved. He explained that the object of the proposed testing would allow some

practical experience to be gained and that later consideration could be given to extending the in-Town operation. He also recorded that experience to date with RTWs had confirmed advantages especially from a conductor's point of view as two thirds of the additional width had been applied to the gangways.

With his colleagues' thoughts in mind about the next cycle of orders, Durrant sought Dalton's advice regarding how best to proceed in order to expedite the necessary official approvals. There were two aspects which Durrant was anxious to clarify: the south London tram conversion and the existing bus routes passing through central London. Plans for the Executive's future requirements could then be swiftly accomplished, once approval had been secured to operate RTWs over routes entirely free of trams.

Dalton's response was that from his position there would be no objection to the operation of RTWs over the south London tram conversion routes but excluding those which continued through to central London. He was, however, aware of the need for such routes to be surveyed although he foresaw little difficulty as there were few pinch points and easy radius turns from one road into another. Dalton suggested a meeting between members of the Executive and the Metropolitan Police as he remained convinced that some central London streets would be totally unsuited for the operation of wider buses.

On 5th April 1950, Durrant, Ottaway and Leonard Hawkins represented the Executive at a meeting held in New Scotland Yard with Dalton, Chief Superintendent Wells and other officials from the Road Research Department, the City of London Police, the Licensing Authority and members of the Metropolitan Police Traffic Department.

The first of the outcomes reiterated that a substantial majority of the tram routes converted to bus operation would be suitable for RTW operation. It was also agreed that everything would be done to assist in deciding the practicability of operating the vehicles in the West End. However, a major difficulty remained regarding the City and Superintendent Hatchett of the City of London Police Force had little optimism for any success. However, those present were made aware that testing was being arranged in an attempt to overcome objections. Agreement was therefore reached for a large scale test to be conducted for all services passing through Notting Hill Gate for one week commencing 15th May and would involve the transfer of RTWs to routes 12, 17, 27A, 28, 31, 46, 52 and 88 during the weekend of 13/14 May. Observations would be undertaken by Dr Smeed of the Road Research Department during the preceding week to ascertain delays and other difficulties while the 7ft 6ins vehicles were in operation and then continue his work during the experiment.

On 25th April a further meeting convened at Scotland Yard under the chairmanship of Chief Superintendent Wells but without participation from members of the Executive. Arising from earlier doubts regarding RTWs operating within the City of London, it was mentioned that the City Commissioner had agreed that the wider vehicles could be used on route 17, this never having featured in any of the Bus Allocation Committee's discussions.

Dr Smeed referred to the test to be held at Notting Hill Gate and stated that the possibility of 8ft bus operation here hinged on any perceived slowing down of traffic which could only be checked by assessing a large number of vehicle movements. This would be achieved by making a significant number of short journeys using four police cars each with an observer whose work would involve noting down the times of the journeys and the duration of any delays at road junctions; both car occupants would be in plain clothes. Following considerable discussion it was agreed that the test would take place over a two-week period. In the first week (9–12 May), no RTWs would operate, manual counts would be taken during four separate hours on the Tuesday, Wednesday and Friday. This sequence would be used during the second week (16–19 May) when RTWs would take to the streets.

On 23rd May, Chief Superintendent Wells received early evaluations of the test conducted, the first using cars on 16, 17 and 19 May from 'F' Division based at Notting Hill Police Station. This found the experiment reasonably successful by recording that wider buses generally did not seriously cause obstruction. However, on some occasions it was noted that when an RTW proceeding west in Notting Hill Gate and making a turn north at Pembridge Road was stopped due to traffic, a slight obstruction could be caused (a) if the vehicle was noted as being too far over the crown of the road resulting in eastbound traffic being reduced from two lanes to one or (b) if the vehicle had not been far enough over the crown of the road, heavy vehicles proceeding west were unable to pass on its nearside. Nevertheless, it was thought that this issue would soon be corrected once the wider vehicles came into general operation and the drivers became fully acquainted with the extra width, some of whom were taking a much wider sweep when turning corners. The Pembridge Road 'turn' was quite acute but no RTWs made contact with the obelisk on the refuge, which periodically occurred when 7ft 6in wide vehicles were in use.

Test 1 Notting Hill Gate
9 May to 19 May 1950

12	Elmers End and Nunhead garages (Croydon allocation remained RT)
17	Riverside (Old Kent Road allocation remained RT)
27A	Holloway, Riverside and Twickenham
28	Chelverton Road and Middle Row
31	Battersea and Chalk Farm
46	Willesden
52	Victoria and Willesden
88	Merton (allocation included brand new RTWs 313/319-322, 324/325)

Test 2 Shaftesbury Avenue
19 June to 1 July 1950

14	Holloway (allocation included brand new RTW 354) and Putney Bridge
19	Battersea and Holloway
22	Battersea and Hackney
38	Leyton
38A	Leyton (Loughton allocation remained STD)

Test 3 Threadneedle Street
3 July to 7 July 1950

6	Hackney and Willesden
8	Clay Hall and Willesden
22	Battersea and Hackney
60	Clay Hall (Cricklewood allocation remained RT)

Except where new vehicles are listed, all buses were on loan from garages around the fleet.
Route numbers shown in bold indicate those which later had a daily allocation of the type.

Also received on 23 May was a report from the Metropolitan Police, compiled by a single officer whose observations had taken place as follows:

Tuesday and Wednesday:
Pembridge Road/Notting Hill Gate and
Notting Hill Gate/Palace Garden Terrace
Wednesday and Friday:
Kensington Church Street/Notting Hill Gate
Tuesday and Friday:
Notting Hill Gate/Pembridge Road

From the graphs submitted there were exceptional periods of congestion both on days of normal bus and RTW operation. These were generally caused by the junction under observation being blocked by one vehicle but never a bus. An example was given citing an event on Friday 19 May when the Notting Hill Gate/Pembridge Road traffic tailed back 325 yards as opposed to the normal 50 yards that was usual for that time of day. A large vehicle turning right into Notting Hill Gate had blocked westbound traffic for a considerable distance.

Also noted by the Met was the congestion caused by parked vehicles, most notably beer wagons delivering to various licensed premises situated in the most awkward places, there being four between Church Street and Pembridge Road.

In conclusion, the observations undertaken during the second week of the experiment showed no marked comparative difference in traffic congestion due to RTW bus operation. Some vehicles were noted to be mounting the pavement during the right turn from Notting Hill Gate into Pembridge Road but this only occurred on the first day.

The Road Research Laboratory also produced a result of its findings as follows:

Route	Estimated Flow on Route (Vehicles per hour)			Mean Journey Time (Minutes)		
	9–12 May	16–19 May	Percentage Change	9–12 May	16–19 May	Percentage Change
N-S Chepstow Place - Kensington Church St	185	177	-4%	4.29	4.19	-2%
S-N Vicarage Gate - Pembridge Road	215	216	0	3.14	3.41	+8%
E-W Queensway - Pembridge Road	669	650	-3%	3.23	3.34	+3%
W-E Ladbroke Grove - Linden Gardens	578	555	-4%	3.22	3.27	-2%
Total inflow to central section	2277	2235	-2%			
Mean Journey Time				3.33	3.42	+3%

1. The total inflow recorded in the Central Area decreased by 2%. The estimated flows were slightly lower on all routes except the northbound example.

2. The number of stationary vehicles in Notting Hill Gate between Pembridge Road and Linden Gardens showed little change.

3. There was a small increase in journey time on three routes and a decrease on the fourth, but none of these changes were considered statistically significant. Averaged over all routes, there was an estimated increase of 3% in the time required to travel through the area, but again this was insignificant.

4. The variability of the time for individual journeys was similar in the two weeks. The variation within the given hour was generally less than that between different hours.

5. The possibility that the RTWs may have slowed down the traffic slightly was deemed too small to be of any significance.

In addition to the tests conducted by the Police and the Road Research Laboratory, the Executive had commissioned an Operational Research Team to investigate the loading and unloading of double deck vehicles of 7ft 6ins and 8ft width. Here the superiority of the 8ft vehicles found that the conductor was on the platform on 93% of occasions compared with 82% on standard width vehicles which allowed the frequent supervision of loading and minimum delay in giving the starting signal. This was due to the wider gangways and platform which facilitated the conductor's movement around the vehicle, a speedier return to the platform and improved fare collection which further reduced delays, it being noted that in only 4% of cases was the conductor observed collecting fares from alighting passengers which compared favourably with the standard vehicles where this occurred in 14% of cases.

The easier circulation of passengers to and from their seats was also noted, this reducing

RTW 263 makes the turn from Notting Hill Gate into Pembridge Road on the largely suburban route 52, which passed through the area on its way to its Victoria terminus. The 52 never had a scheduled allocation of RTWs after the end of the trial. *London Transport Museum*

overcrowding around the vehicle while the increased platform width allowed the conductor to stand clear of the passenger flow with small delays being absorbed and reduced interruption to the passengers.

Another meeting held in the Commissioner's Office of Scotland Yard primarily discussed the findings of the Notting Hill Gate test about which Dr Smeed recorded that he was very satisfied with there being no major slowing down and certainly no major obstructions.

Burnell, one of the three LTE representatives at the meeting, stated that the RTWs came from all parts of London to reach Notting Hill Gate for the tests and the Executive had taken the precaution of issuing a list of places where there might have been pinch-points; a warning had also been issued to tram drivers. In the event, no difficulties were encountered and RTW drivers had no adverse comments to make.

Durrant commented upon the improvement in loading and unloading stating that, from a conductor's point of view, it was clear that the extra inches on the width were more important than on the length.

It was then time for those present at the meeting to agree upon a location for the next test and immediately Burnell reported that neither Streatham nor Loughton garages would be available. Mr D Counihan, the third of the Executive's representatives stated that 530 RTWs would be required if the test were to be held at the suggested location of Knightsbridge, there being 330 currently available. Should Oxford Street be chosen, 660 would be required from Marble Arch to Portman Street, 761 from Bond Street to Oxford Circus, 377 from Oxford Street to St Giles. It was agreed that the next test would be held using Shaftesbury Avenue.

The 28 was one of the routes in the first width trials and never had RTWs again after its short period with them in May 1950. RTW 165, on loan from route 112 at Palmers Green, is seen at Wandsworth. *Alan B. Cross, The Bus Archive*

RTW 42 was on loan from Alperton when photographed in Kensington Church Street in the week of the first batch of availability trials, centred on Notting Hill Gate in May 1950. It carries blinds transferred from the STL buses normally used on the route and the front one is of the first style of restricted display with the route number centralised above the place names served, a style that predated the entry into service of the first RTWs. As we shall see, RTWs were to return to the 31 at the end of 1950. *Alan B. Cross, The Bus Archive*

RTW 113 working from Riverside is followed by RTW 123 working from Twickenham in this view. The 27A was mostly STL-worked before the trials, but was converted to RTL afterwards, renumbered 27 in 1952 and never again saw RTWs except as unscheduled workings later on in the 27's history. Prior to 1952 the route number 27 was used for the Sunday only version and so did not see RTWs in the trial period. *Alan B. Cross, The Bus Archive*

RTW 76 is seen at the still-extant 1898 Coronet Cinema building at the junction of Hillgate Street and Notting Hill Gate. Renamed the Gaumont shortly before this photograph was taken, it reverted to its original name in the 1970s when it was sold by the Rank Organisation. Route 17 paralleled route 7 between the London Bridge terminus and Marble Arch and then continued along Bayswater Road instead of Edgware Road. It was a casualty of the 1958 bus strike. Its week with RTWs in May 1950 was the only period of RTW operation on the route. *Alan B. Cross, The Bus Archive*

Routes 12 and 88 in the first set of width trials were two of the routes involved in the trials that never saw RTWs again, thereby seeing the type for just five days. Both paralleled tram services for part of their length and this is evident in the view of RTW 306. Route 88 paralleled trams between Vauxhall Bridge and Tooting. Route 12, which paralleled trams between Westminster Bridge and Peckham, is represented by RTW 146 in one of a series of views from Alan Cross taken at Notting Hill Gate. The 12 also had an allocation of buses from Croydon, but these remained RT as all that garage's journeys terminated at Oxford Circus. *Alan B. Cross, The Bus Archive*

RTW 133 is seen at the top end of Shaftesbury Avenue outside the Palace Theatre and just before route 38's turn into Charing Cross Road. Two unidentified RTWs follow it on routes 22 and 14.

Dr Smeed was anxious to conduct a test involving the standard width vehicles in the fortnight prior to the RTWs taking to the road thus allowing for the daily observations and the number of cars used being reduced by half. He required all of the work to be undertaken by the end of July so as not to be affected by school holidays as he considered the City test of greater importance and that it should take place immediately after that in Shaftesbury Avenue. This move was wholeheartedly supported by Burnell, who stated that the Executive operated on a 15-year cycle regarding the placing of orders for buses and naturally a change to the dimensions of the new fleet, then in the process of being delivered, would require swift action.

A suggestion for the use of Threadneedle Street for the City test had been made previously but there was a note of caution regarding the use of RTWs in Fenchurch Street due to road works. Despite this detail, an agreement was finally reached for the tests of RTWs in Shaftesbury Avenue to occur from 19th June to 1st July and from 3rd July to 7th July in Threadneedle Street with observations of standard vehicles taking place in Shaftesbury Avenue from 12th June for one week followed by a further week's observations from 3rd July. However, in consequence of the operation of RTWs on Route 22 in connection with the City test, the second week of observations involving standard width buses in Shaftesbury Avenue was rescheduled for week commencing 10th July.

As previously agreed RTWs were allocated to the Shaftesbury Avenue routes for two weeks from 19th June 1950. Timed journeys were made during these weeks, the previous week and 12th–14th July. During each of the four weeks observations were made on Wednesdays,

Thursdays and Fridays during the hours of 10-11am, 12-1pm 2-3pm and 4-5pm. The five routes running the length of Shaftesbury Avenue (14,19,22,38 and 38A (Leyton only)) provided a flow of about 80 buses per hour in each direction, other traffic mainly comprised private cars and taxis and a few heavy commercial vehicles. The distance under surveillance was 0.3mile and despite being a no waiting thoroughfare, vehicles frequently stopped during restricted hours at the many shops, theatres and restaurants.

Journey times and times stopped *en route* between the refuges at the point of entry to and exit from Shaftesbury Avenue were recorded by a plain clothes police observer travelling in a police car that kept within the normal traffic flow; a stopwatch being provided; the journeys were made continuously with the car turning at Piccadilly and Cambridge Circuses. At these points and at the same time other police observers counted traffic entering and leaving Shaftesbury Avenue vehicles being classified as buses, taxis and other vehicles.

During the first half of the experiment, the taxi drivers took industrial action with a result

that observations were for one week with and one week without the RTWs while the strike was in progress. A strike by some Smithfield drivers at the end of June had little impact on Shaftesbury Avenue traffic.

An issue considered during the testing was the effect of the extra width of RTWs when overtaking which was found to cause no problems other than where a taxi rank existed in the centre of the road.

Some salient points from the Shaftesbury Avenue experiment were listed in the published report as being:

1.   The end of the strike by London taxi drivers on 26th June resulted in an increase in the traffic flow in Shaftesbury Avenue and caused a significant reduction in the speed of the traffic.

2.   There was little or no difference between the journey time of the RTWs while the taxis were on strike when compared with the narrower vehicles.

3.   During the RTWs' second week, journey times were noted as being longer although the difference was of doubtful significance.

RTW 157 is seen working from Putney Bridge garage during the second set of width trials, which included route 14. RTWs were to return to this service a few years later, as we shall see. Putney Bridge shared the route with Holloway, which also received RTWs for the trial period. *Alan B. Cross, The Bus Archive*

RTWs also worked on the 14A, a summer Sunday service to Hampton Court, where RTW 179 is seen on 25th June 1950, the only day the route had the type, as it was withdrawn by the time RTWs worked regularly on the 14, into which it was absorbed. As mentioned earlier, Hampton Court was the farthest south-west that RTWs reached in normal passenger service, even though it was for just one day with Kingston having that honour otherwise. Putney Bridge garage used the ten vehicles of the type already there for the 85, and these were joined by 16 buses loaned from Palmers Green for the period. *J H Aston*

Route 19, on which RTW 259 is seen in Trinity Road, was also in the second set of width trials and never saw RTWs on weekdays again, though Battersea was scheduled to use them on Sundays between October 1952 and May 1954. In recent times the route, unchanged in central London since the trials, received LTs measuring nearly 37ft long and 8ft 3ins wide and travelling over roads that in most cases have seen little change since 1950. It raises the question of what all the fuss was about. The 22 did get its own daily allocation of RTWs again; they returned to this route in August 1951. RTW 294 is seen at the route's Putney Heath terminus. *W.R. Legg and J. H. Aston*

From the Shaftesbury Avenue Test the RTWs moved seamlessly to Threadneedle Street to operate on routes 6, 6A, 8, 22 and 60, for which the City of London Police provided three observers, a driver and a test car.

Threadneedle Street, divided into two sections by its junction with Old Broad Street, was considered a narrow and busy road with mixed traffic. In addition to the RTWs allocated to the test routes, standard width vehicles operating on routes 7, 11 and 13 (and occasionally route 76) joined Threadneedle Street at the Old Broad Street junction and travelled in one direction only to the Bank.

Observations were made throughout the periods 9am to 11am and 2pm to 4pm. Stationed at Old Broad Street, two observers recorded the flow of buses and of all other vehicles (except pedal cycles). Simultaneously the police car made repeated test runs along Threadneedle Street in both directions.

It was necessary to reject some of the data collected while the RTWs were undergoing their third and final test due to a number of incidents having altered local conditions. On 5th July there was so much congestion in Bishopsgate, north of its junction with Threadneedle Street, that vehicles travelling east could not freely leave the area, invalidating all data collected. During the morning of 6th July heavy rain reduced road speed and, as this became the only rainy period experienced during the test, the observations were rejected. On the afternoon of 7th July the traffic signals at the Bank complex failed and the intersection was controlled by police officers resulting in a failure to provide comparable conditions when the standard width vehicles returned the following week.

After discarding the data collected during the abnormal periods, the remainder formed a reasonable picture for the whole week which, when compared with the results achieved showed no significant difference in the mean journey times. In conclusion there were few considerations relating to the City test.

Uniformed bus inspectors patrolled the length of Threadneedle Street, a move no doubt initiated by the Executive as their job was to stop any jams occurring that involved RTWs and to discourage drivers from 'crawling' if they were in advance of the scheduled times. The London Transport bus inspectors did not put in appearances during the second week.

The roadworks and one-way working in Fenchurch Street during both weeks were thought to have affected traffic in Threadneedle Street where conditions were likely to have been somewhat abnormal during the experiment. The Road Research team found that journey times slightly increased during the operation of the RTWs. However, none of the changes in journey times were recorded as being statistically significant.

Bishopsgate is the setting for this view of RTW 314. The 8A did not serve Threadneedle Street but was included in the third trials because its buses came from the parent route. *Prince Marshall, The Bus Archive*

All reports regarding the result of the three trials were completed by September 1950 but there appeared no haste in advising the Executive of the results.

On 3rd November Burnell wrote to Assistant Commissioner Dalton at New Scotland Yard to emphasise the Executive's concerns regarding the delay in receiving authority to operate 8ft wide buses in the Inner London Area. He also reminded Dalton of the need to place quickly further orders for new buses and also sought permission to operate RTWs on Route 39 for

which an application had already been submitted, this decision in no way affecting the outcome of the tests.

However, the results of first two tests were still being analysed which culminated in a memorandum from the Commissioner's Office recording non-acceptance of the Executive's suggestion that improved performance at bus stops compensated for the disadvantages of the extra width. Nevertheless, Met Police officers placed on record that it was no longer possible to continue the complete exclusion of the RTW

from the inner London area. The City Police had yet to be consulted, although it was known that the views of the City Police Traffic Department equated with those of the Met.

On 14th November, Dalton sent the results of the testing to the Licensing Authority for Public Service Vehicles in the Metropolitan Area, from which a letter conveying the judgment of all parties was sent to the Executive on the 23rd. Burnell was now charged with reviewing the Inner London services with a view to using the RTWs to the best advantage.

Beyond 500

Durrant recorded during a meeting of the Informal Road Service Committee on 5th July 1950 that if further routes were authorised in the near future for operation by RTWs there could be an increase in their number over and above the 500 currently in production. The bodies would have to be built by firms other than Leyland owing to the existing contractual commitments of that company. Consequently, some delay was anticipated in connection with design work and retool, for which additional costs were expected. Durrant then undertook to report upon the situation to Valentine in his capacity as a member of the Executive.

Valentine replied stating that he doubted whether there was an early prospect of ascertaining the additional 8ft vehicles the Board would be permitted to operate. Durrant responded by recording that the earliest possible date would be January 1952 as it would take this time to redesign the RT3 and make the necessary arrangements on the production line. The design work would be intensive with only the two side frame structures remaining unaltered.

There followed a note of caution whereby, if such a path were followed, then inevitably the work then being undertaken relating to the 'new 62 seater bus' would be delayed and this Durrant thought unacceptable. He also added that additional orders for 8ft buses from Leyland could not be placed before January 1952 due to Weymann and Park Royal having been assured of their delivery requirements up to that date.

In addition to the redesign of the body, the AEC chassis would also require revision but there was no doubt that this could be achieved in the indicated time space. After the end of December 1951, it would be possible for Leyland to be contracted to provide the balance of 25%

complete double-deck buses as permitted by the AEC contract but this would only provide 425 vehicles up to the end of the current replacement cycle (188 in 1952, 218 in 1953 and 19 in 1954). Durrant saw an alternative that would embrace an offer made by Leyland whereby the company's drawings for body construction would be handed over to other manufacturers resulting in either Park Royal or Weymann or both turning production over to the 'Leyland' 8ft body. This action would involve a comprehensive revision of the AEC chassis in order to accept that body.

Another report, issued on 21st June 1950, examined the operating costs of the RTWs, each costing approximately £360 more than an RT to build. However, it was recognised that if Park Royal Vehicles or Weymann, and perhaps AEC, were required to alter their output to the production of wider vehicles, the cost would increase further and some interruption of the production lines would occur while new jigs and tools were brought into use. Higher costs were considered inevitable when compared with the first batch of 500, for which the increased width of the adapted Leyland chassis had been accomplished using longer axles to which slightly heavier duty wheels had been fitted. The structure of the standard Leyland body had been modified to take wider panels at the front, rear and across the roof, the dimensions of the driver's windscreen and the rear window were also increased and there had been a slight rearrangement of the staircase to suit the widened saloons.

Operating costs of the wider vehicles were given as approximately £40 per annum above that of the standard RT or £20,000 for the whole 500. The larger tyres fitted to the class were thought capable of providing additional mileage

over the RT, these showing an increase of £9.00 per annum. Other operating costs were deemed unchanged by the introduction of the RTW. Drivers initially trained on RTs were given a further two hours instruction on the RTW, but fortunately some drivers had already received their initial training on the type.

Costs for maintenance of the RTWs could only be estimated. The most significant chassis alteration was the extension of the axles and provision had already been made for the higher cost of these components. Both the RTLs and the RTWs were powered by Leyland's 9.8 litre 6-cylinder engine. Many of the body components were larger, as previously recorded, but these were only considered in need of replacement following accident damage. The vehicles did have a larger superficial area to be painted and larger floor areas and staircase to be retreated and retreaded. The difference in unladen weights between an RTL with composite body and an RTW with an all-metal body was 5cwt, which could be scaled down to 3½cwt representing an increase of 2.2%. In view of the increase, additional mechanical wear was expected and the same 2% was applied to Chiswick and garage engineering costs.

The introduction of the RTW resulted in no changes at Chiswick but plans for the new works at Aldenham, specifically for the body lifting shop, had to be adjusted to allow for a wider vehicle, resulting in a larger space and a cost increase of £10,000. This would later prove to have been a wise investment when the eight-foot wide Routemasters came on stream.. The new overhaul works had been designed for a fleet of 10,000 vehicles so that here the additional expenditure per vehicle was deemed insignificant anyway.

Garage accommodation for the RTWs was envisaged to be to the same standard of amenity as for the RTs. However, it was appreciated that some of the fleet was still parked in the open and the influx of the wider vehicles would increase this number. Additional garage accommodation was in the process of being provided with a further increase than would have been the case had the double deck fleet remained at 7ft 6ins. The capital cost of housing an RTW was estimated as £40 more than a 7ft 6ins vehicle.

On 12th October 1950, a meeting was held at which Durrant and Ottaway represented the Executive, with Messrs W R Black of Park Royal Vehicles and B Homfray Davies of Weymann. In opening discussion, Durrant explained that the successful trials of 8ft wide buses through certain central London thoroughfares had widened the prospect for securing approval for the extended use of these vehicles. Due to the benefits of the wider body, the Executive's operating managers wanted to take the earliest advantage of adding to the fleet of 8ft buses. It had therefore become necessary to give immediate consideration to the possibilities of changing future production of RT3 bodies to an 8ft design. With the beginning of 1952 already recorded as the earliest date possible, the question remained as to whether the necessary preparations could be made for a production switch then or shortly after.

The Chiswick drawing office had undertaken the majority of the work in the design of the RT3 body, but priority commitments dictated that Chiswick could only act in a supervisory capacity for the design for the wider bus. Durrant stressed that, in spite of the need to treat the changeover as a matter of urgency, it was essential that design work should be carried out in the same detail as that for the RT3.

A further meeting was called. This took place on 26th October when Durrant and his Works Manager, J W Wicks, met with Black and Homfray Davies. Here Durrant was able to report that enquiries had been made of consulting designers Messrs Wilson & Rodger who were known to be a reputable organisation and fully capable of undertaking the design work for the 8ft wide buses. The company had confirmed that it should be possible to complete detail drawings by May 1951 and then follow on to the completion of assembly drawings within the following two or three months.

From discussions that followed, it appeared probable that Park Royal and Weymann would be able to produce the necessary jigs, tools or alterations thereto in order for the production of 8ft bodies to commence by January 1952.

An early significant point stressed that it was highly desirable to avoid the introduction of a further non-interchangeable chassis as a result of switching production to the 8ft body and that AEC had undertaken to redesign the 3RT chassis to ensure that it was interchangeable with the Leyland chassis in respect of body mounting.

The contracts with Park Royal Vehicles and Weymann provided that they would manufacture the whole of the Executive's requirements for RT3 bodies during the currency of their current contracts, which were only capable of termination following two year's notice. With production for 1951 already committed, there was no possibility of purchasing further 8ft wide vehicles during that year, it having been made clear that no further deliveries from Leyland could be made above the order for 500.

With 1952 still being cited as the year when a changeover in production could occur, three possibilities presented themselves:

(1) That a further order should be placed with Leyland for complete 8ft vehicles. The number ordered being restricted to 25% of chassis requirements as previously recorded.

(2) To take advantage of the offer made by Leyland to release drawings and special tools for the production of their design of body so that it might be manufactured by others.

(3) To find a means whereby the design of the RT3 body to 8ft width could be undertaken to permit production at or around the end of 1951.

Obviously the third option was the best of the three, AEC and the two body construction companies having agreed that the changeover should be made simultaneously. The outcome of this occurring by the end of 1951 would see a further 1,780 8ft wide RTs added to the fleet, making a total of 2,280 at the end of the current replacement cycle.

The three officers were of the opinion that the 8ft wide bus constituted an important advance in design and that with regard to the vehicle itself, its merits in traffic operation significantly outweighed any disadvantages.

It was therefore recommended that commencing in 1952 or as soon after as possible, the supply of new double-deckers should be switched to the 8ft wide design by introducing the necessary changes at AEC, Park Royal and Weymann. The proposal would still permit a proportion of chassis being ordered from Leyland since they would be interchangeable with the Park Royal or Weymann bodies insofar as mounting was concerned.

However, at the Executive Conference held in November 1950 it was agreed that no changes would be made to the current manufacturing arrangements to increase the number of 8ft wide buses in the present cycle of replacement.

Berlin Visit

In September 1950 two brand new RTWs, 421 and 422, were loaned to the Board of Trade and prepared for a trade fair in Berlin, involving a 700-mile road trip to the western half of the then divided city. They were driven there and back by three London Transport engineers, wearing bus driver's uniforms, so that they could deal with running repairs and maintenance on the journey, which crossed the Channel by boat from Dover, setting off on Sunday 24th September. On the Continent the buses travelled by way of Liege, Brussels, Hanover and Cologne. On arrival in Berlin, the engineers instructed German bus drivers so that they could drive the RTWs in passenger service there during the period of the fair. Both buses returned on 20th October and entered service from Chalk Farm on route 31 in November.

London Transport put out a press release on 8th November announcing that the first of these (RTW 421) had just started work on the route. It said that the bus would be 'eagerly looked out for by youthful spotters' but unfortunately the release gave the number incorrectly as RTW 41.

RTW 422 at Chiswick ready for its trip with RTW 421 to West Berlin, that part of the German capital that was under the occupation of Britain, France and America following Germany's defeat at the end of the Second World War. The buses were fitted with an extra rear view mirror on the nearside wing.
London Transport Museum

RTW 422 (left) and RTW 421 (right) at the YMCA Windmill on their way to the Berlin trade fair. The Windmill was on the A2 autobahn near Beckum which led to Berlin. It closed in 1937 and was opened as a restaurant in 1939. After the Second World War the British army confiscated the windmill and set up a British canteen, using it as the YMCA until closure in 1971. *Jim Hawkins collection*

London Buses at Windmill

Below left: RTW 421 seen during its time offering free rides to West Berliners. If ever a bus was justifiably described as a box on wheels, it must surely be the vintage local double decker about to overtake it.

The two RTWs were the only members of their class to receive GB plates. Both began service in London on routes 31 and 39 from Chalk Farm garage in November 1950. Both buses retained their original bodies until withdrawal. *London Transport Museum*

Through the Heart of London

Introduction of RTWs on outer suburban routes had ended with the 114 conversion, which was completed in October 1950. Before formal consent for central London operation was given by the Met and City police, approval for 8ft wide buses to be used on route 74 (Camden Town to Putney Heath via Marble Arch and Earls Court) was received. The route received RTWs from 23rd August 1950. It ran along none of the three thoroughfares that were the main focus of the three width trials but was the first use of RTWs in central London following these. The conversion took fleet numbers in service up to RTW 428 and the buses were the last of the type to enter service as new with restricted front blinds (though all RTWs were delivered from Leyland with the masking in place). Putney Bridge was the sole operating garage of the route at the time and the RTWs were also used on the long summer Sunday 14A (Hornsey Rise to Hampton Court) until this route ceased at the end of the 1952 summer timetable.

In October, after completion of the 74, Chalk Farm received its first RTWs for route 31. Battersea followed in November for its allocation on the same route. Then, following the November go-ahead for the conversion of routes that more fully penetrated the central area, the 39, running between Camden Town and Southfields via Trafalgar Square and operated by the same two garages, was changed over. It was these two services that completed the allocation of new RTWs when RTW 500 started work at Battersea in December 1950, twenty months after RTW 1 had entered service.

January 1951 saw no major changes in the RTW fleet as such, but was significant in that a large part of the tram network was swept away, paving the way for RTWs to venture into south London more readily. February 1951, however,

saw a large movement towards the centre. The isolated RTW contingent at Bromley, after only six months there, was swapped with RTs from Willesden, and took up residence on the 8 and 8A – two of the trials routes – on 21st February. The Clay Hall contribution was obtained by sweeping Palmers Green and route 112 clean of RTWs in exchange for RTLs, plus a contribution gleaned from Seven Kings's 139 route. RTWs spare from the 8/8A allocation on Saturdays were used on route 60.

Enfield lost its small batch for route 144A in March to increase RTWs at Putney Bridge. 11th April saw even more changes, with the conversion of the famous route 11 plus the 6 and 6A. For Dalston's large share of the 11 all the RTWs were from Leyton and Upton Park, with a large contribution from Harrow Weald, plus some from Putney Bridge. On Saturdays, Dalston used eight RTWs spare from its route 11 allocation on route 9. Riverside (Hammersmith) gained its share for the 11 also from Harrow Weald, as did Willesden and Hackney for the 6 and 6A. This wiped Harrow Weald clear, and still left a deficit. So Edgware swapped some of its RTWs to Riverside, plus some to Putney Bridge to restore its allocation. All these buses were replaced by RTs or RTLs from the garages involved, or through three-way swaps to keep RT and RTL allocations separate. Willesden also used RTWs on route 52 on Sundays, when it had 21 of the type spare from its weekday duties.

At a Bus Allocation Committee meeting on 26th April 1951, a participant representing the operating staff asked if it was intended that the RTWs would operate permanently in the inner area. He mentioned 'certain deficiences' in the vehicles. These issues were unspecified in the minutes but the main one would probably have

been the heavier steering of the type compared to RTs, especially on busy routes when heavily laden. Mr Burnell replied that the 8ft wide buses were most suitable for the inner area by reason of their wider gangways and there was no intention of moving them. Durrant's personal assistant stated that the Executive did not accept that the buses were inferior to the RT.

Another major swap-around came one week after that meeting, when on 2nd May West Green lost its entire allocation to Tottenham for route 76 and the interworked 34B, which also robbed Barking and Alperton. After a brief absence, RTWs returned to route 144 on Sundays following this conversion, only to be taken off again not long after. Southall and Alperton also sent RTWs to Willesden for the 46, receiving RTLs in return. 1st August 1951 saw the 22 re-equipped with RTWs, at Hackney and Battersea, the buses coming from Seven Kings, Southall and Barking, who got RTLs in return. Southall lost its remainder on the 15th of the month, in company with Alperton and Shepherd's Bush, when Upton Park had its second period with RTWs, this time with a large number for the 15 and Sunday route 23A. For a time, route 129 also used RTWs from this allocation on Saturdays and Sundays. From October 1951 Edgware's RTWs on routes 140 and 142 were dispersed to other RTW garages as and when replacement buses became available.

The move from suburban routes to central London ones was largely complete, though the pioneer route 41 continued to be operated by the type on a daily basis. By May 1952, Hackney's 106 was also operated with RTWs, partially on Mondays to Saturdays and fully on Sundays. Special suburban works services 34B and 100 also carried on with RTWs using buses off the 76 and 15 routes respectively.

Route 74 did not penetrate the centre of the West End but came close to it. It was the first RTW route to serve areas other than those in the suburbs following the width trials. RTWs started to arrive at Putney Bridge garage for it on 23rd August 1950 and the conversion from RT was completed on 21 September. RTW 426 is seen at South Kensington when fresh into service. The design of the ornate traffic light pole was unique to the Royal Borough of Kensington. *Capital Transport*

Below: Routes 31, 39 and 74 were the only central London routes to have a regular allocation using RTWs from new and Chalk Farm routes 31 and 39 had buses with full blinds from the start. All RTWs were delivered from Leyland with the red-painted masking front and back for restricted blind displays. The first to have this removed were Berlin visitors 421 and 422, followed by 443-457 and 459-500 for CF. All other RTWs lost the masking at their first overhaul, with one exception (RTW 52) which will be covered later. Battersea garage's RTW 471 is seen entering Kilburn High Road. *Ron Wellings*

Opposite: The last of the class, RTW 500, also allocated to Battersea, is seen at Victoria. It was licensed for service in December 1950 along with 481/482/484/488-490 and 492-499 shared between B and CF, the gaps in this series having entered service the previous month. Routes 31, 39 and 74 all retained RTWs until 1965, though the 39 allocation was only part-RTW from 1961. The normal northern terminus of the 39 was Camden Gardens, a short distance from Camden Town Station, so it is possible that an incorrect ultimate destination is displayed in this view. *Alan B. Cross, The Bus Archive*

The 8 and 8A were next, both of which had been part of the width trials, and were converted on 21st February 1951, Willesden's buses coming from Bromley and Clay Hall's buses coming from Seven Kings. This view of Clay Hall garage's RTW 166 was taken on 2nd June 1953, Coronation Day, when services in central London were curtailed to avoid the processional route, in this case at the north-eastern end of Shaftesbury Avenue. RTW 166 had taken part in all three of the width trials, when it had been loaned to Middle Row, Putney Bridge and Hackney respectively. *Alan B. Cross, The Bus Archive*

Most RTWs had their destination blind boxes changed from restricted displays to full form during their first overhaul at Aldenham during 1952-1954. Some however had this done before overhaul, as evidenced by RTW 205 with cream upper deck windows at London Bridge. This bus went for overhaul in November 1953. *Alan B. Cross, The Bus Archive*

On Saturdays, spare RTWs from the Clay Hall allocation were used on route 60 (another of the width trial routes). RTW 368 was delivered in July 1950 (after the trials) and is seen at Trafalgar Square the following year. *Robert Mack*

The famous, though now sadly curtailed, route 11 was an obvious candidate for a permanent allocation of RTWs. RTW 118 moved from Leyton to Dalston garage for the route on the occasion of its conversion to the type on 11th April 1951 and is seen outside St Martin-in-the-Fields at Charing Cross. Route 11 had a scheduled allocation of 67 buses at the time: 49 from Dalston and 18 from Riverside. *John L. Smith*

On Saturdays, Dalston used spare RTWs from the route 11 allocation on its share of route 9. Dalston at no time had enough for their full share and at first its RTWs served on the route alongside RTs. The RTW allocation changed to RTL for two years from 1954. *Alan B. Cross, The Bus Archive*

Another busy route that called for RTWs was the 6, which at that time ran from Kensal Rise Station to Leyton Town Hall. The 6 was converted to RTW on the same date as the 11 and was worked with an allocation of 30 RTWs from Willesden and 25 from Hackney, the latter allocation being shared with the 6A which deviated from the 6 westbound at Aldwych to run to and terminate at Waterloo. RTW 226, seen soon after its first overhaul, is very recognisably at Trafalgar Square. *Robert Mack*

RTW 333 moved to Tottenham as part of the conversion of route 76 to the type. Victoria was its southern terminus at the time and this view at Parliament Square also shows a vintage FX1 taxi. In Monday to Friday peak hours some RTWs from its allocation were used on works service 34B on various sections of its route between Walthamstow Crooked Billet and Brimsdown Power Station before or after journeys on the donor service. Direct journeys to Brimsdown from Victoria displayed 76 throughout. *Roy Marshall*

Route 34B was a long standing special service for workers at Brimsdown Power Station in Enfield. It had no allocation of its own, taking the buses it needed from route 76's allocation. *Alan B. Cross, The Bus Archive*

Some route 76 journeys operated direct from the southern terminus at Victoria to Brimsdown, from where they returned as a 34B (though sometimes the conductor did not change the blinds from 76). This photo shows the later style of rear upper deck rainstrip fitted on overhaul at Aldenham Works. *Mick Webber collection*

On 4th May 1951 the Festival of Britain on London's South Bank opened and three RTW routes were among those that served it, the 6A, the 76 and also the 46, the last of which joined the other two on the 2nd of that month, ready for the big event. This had an allocation of 22 buses from Willesden garage, joining scheduled allocations of 30 for route 6 and 28 for route 8. *Alan B. Cross, The Transport Archive*

Route 15 was next, on 15th August 1951, along with the Beckton gas works service 100, which took buses from the route 15 allocation. The 100 had six widely-spaced journeys on Mondays to Fridays, five on Saturdays and three on Sundays. *Ron Wellings and Alan B. Cross, The Bus Archive*

Sunday only route 23A (Becontree Heath to Wormwood Scrubs) was converted at the same time as route 15 as there were enough spare buses from that for the purpose. RTW 72 is seen in the City. The 23A was withdrawn between Ladbroke Grove and Wormwood Scrubs in October of the following year. It retained RTWs until its withdrawal in 1958. *Alan B. Cross, The Bus Archive*

London Transport may not have found enough suitable central London routes as the next route to receive the type was the 106. However, its heavy demand no doubt warranted 8ft wide buses, albeit running alongside RTs from Leyton garage. It ran between Becontree and Finsbury Park and continued to do so throughout its time with RTWs. RTW 323 is in Burdett Road, Limehouse. *Allen T. Smith, The Bus Archive*

Settling in the Centre

From the early 1950s RTWs provided a distinctive touch to central London. They were a little different, but very much at home on the Capital's busiest routes. New tasks came their way as the fifties progressed. Monday to Saturday route 18B, Brent Station to London Bridge, and the Sunday version of route 18, which ran all the way from Edgware Station to London Bridge, were converted gradually to RTW beginning in May 1954. The scheduled allocation for these was 18 buses from Willesden garage, which came by way of vehicles released after completion of the first RTW overhaul cycle and fleet spares.

Withdrawal of the wartime 2RT2s from Putney Bridge in February 1955 brought replacements for route 14 in the shape of RTWs from surpluses around the fleet. That month was also to see the early withdrawal of the post-war STDs, which had been delivered just three years before the first RTWs. Major cuts in services on the 16th of that month in response to increasing car usage had allowed this. The Cravens RTs, which were delivered about the same time as the RTWs, followed in 1956. From 2nd May 1956 the Saturday allocation on route 9 from Dalston garage was again converted to RTW, the type staying on this day until 17 May 1963.

Routes 18 and 18B had a gradual conversion to RTW between May 1954 and the early part of 1955, using buses ex-overhaul and spares from around the fleet. The 18 (which at that time ran between Edgware and Wembley Empire Pool) had a long Sunday extension from Wembley to London Bridge and it was on this day only that RTWs worked on it. The 18B, starting from Brent (now Brent Cross) station, served the section between Craven Park and London Bridge on Mondays to Saturdays. *Photomatic and Norman Rayfield, 2RT2 Bus Preservation Group.*

Spare buses were also found to convert Putney garage's share of the 14, one of the routes that had been included in the second set of width trials. They worked on the route, always alongside RTs from Holloway garage, until 1963 when the 14 was the first RTW route to be converted to RM operation. RTW 417 is seen at Oxford Road, Putney, in 1958. *Mick Webber collection*

Route 8B (Old Ford to Alperton) was a Sunday only renumbering of route 8 that was introduced with route changes from 16th October 1957. It was renumbered on this day as part of that route's revisions during the week. The 8B began with 10 RTWs and RML 3 from route 8's allocation at Willesden garage and an unspecified number of RTWs from the 8A allocation at Clay Hall (which moved to Bow garage in November 1959). During the May to November 1959 operation of the first production RMs on central London bus routes, these also appeared on it. By 1960, the 8B allocation from Willesden had increased to 24, presumably with a reduction in Bow's unspecified share. This Sunday only route lasted until 18 November 1964.

New route 39A (Waterloo to Southfields) was introduced with RTWs on 12th January 1958 (Sunday only route) but was withdrawn, among many other services, on 26th November 1958 following the very damaging six-week bus strike that summer. During this, those who could switched to cars or taxis, often sharing, and many of those who could not took to bikes. London's commuters found alternative ways of getting to work, their workplaces usually being within reasonable walking distance from an Underground or main line railway station.

Dalston's allocation on route 9 was re-converted to RTW on Saturdays only from 2nd May 1956, having been operated with these buses on this day between April 1951 and March 1954. It seemed an obvious candidate for the wider vehicles but never had a Monday to Friday allocation of RTWs. RTW 189 is seen at Hammersmith's Butterwick bus station, which opened in 1958 and was adjacent to the ones that exist today. *Michael Dryhurst*

New route 8B was introduced to replace route 8 on Sundays. The 8 had an extension from Kingsbury to Wembley Empire Pool on Mondays to Saturdays and a further extension to Wembley Trading Estate during Monday to Friday peak hours. The Sunday 8 had previously worked to Alperton and the fact that the extended weekday service broke away from the Sunday pattern just a short distance to serve the trading estate in peak hours hardly justified renumbering. *Peter Mitchell*

Route 39A was a new Sunday only route introduced on 12th January 1958. It ran between Southfields and Victoria with an extension on Sunday afternoons for the benefit of visitors to St Thomas's Hospital opposite County Hall. It did not survive the aftermath of the bus strike that year and was withdrawn on 26th November along with the Sunday service on route 39. *Norman Rayfield, 2RT2 Bus Preservation Group*

Willesden garage's RTW 52 was used to experiment with fluorescent lighting in its front blind box. It was because of this that it retained a restricted blind display until long after other buses had changed over to full ones. This photo dates from after its first overhaul in 1953, when all other double deckers were being outshopped with full blind displays. It is possible RTW 52 kept the fluorescent lighting and restricted blind display until it was taken in as a works float in October 1956. No other buses of the RT family were so fitted and indeed the first red buses to have such lighting were the XAs, though the timing of the experiment suggests it was being considered for the RM. *Bruce Jenkins*

RTW 395 with BESI plate in place passes one of the special BESI scanning posts, which were designed and made at London Transport's Parsons Green Works and Buildings Department. This photo was taken at Shoreditch. *London Transport Museum*

By the late 1950s traffic congestion, especially in central London, was having such deleterious effects on bus operation that traditional methods of control involving inspectors and dedicated telephone lines for communication were inadequate. From early 1958 London Transport began trials with electronic equipment using roadside scanners to monitor passing buses and transmit the information to a central point, where controllers could compare the data received with the schedules and take appropriate action to regulate the service. The project had been launched to the press shortly before Christmas 1957. The control room for the system (Bus Electronic Scanning Indicator – or BESI) was initially at the 55 Broadway headquarters but it later moved to an office above Mansion House Underground station.

The earliest trials were carried out on RTW route 74, which then ran between Camden Town and Putney Heath. At first there were four scanners in each direction along the route. The scanner, which was mounted on a pole, read plates with reflective studs fixed on the nearside of the bus between the cream band and upper deck windows. Various configurations of studs were arranged on two plates to read the route number and the running number in binary code. Initially the two plates were one above the other but during the next three years they were arranged horizontally in the same straight line. By 1961 the system had developed to have four reflective panels on the route plate providing for fifteen route codes and seven on the running number plate, which in binary provided for up to 127 numbers.

By early 1961 BESI had been extended to include six more routes, namely 6, 6A, 13, 28, 31 and 73. A specially designed concrete post was employed to house the scanners and during the next few years there was some adjustment to the routes equipped. The 9, 11 and 22 are known to have been included. Eight routes were in operation by 1965: 6, 6A, 13, 30, 73, 74, 74A and 74B. Many of the routes concerned were RTW operated initially, with BESI equipment being fitted to replacement types as the RTWs were gradually withdrawn.

By 1965, a total of 232 buses were reported as fitted with BESI reflectors, monitored by 43 roadside scanners. BESI lasted until 1976 when the whole system was withdrawn, having been overtaken by advancing technology involving radio communication such as CARLA.

1958

1958 saw a contraction in bus provision throughout the fleet, especially after the strike. Enough RTWs became available through the re-entry to service of the Aldenham Works float at the end of the overhaul round for Chalk Farm to convert route 24 to RTW operation.

Also, in November 1958, the big shake-up implementing service reductions after the strike saw the complete withdrawal of Sunday-only cross-London route 23A, which took its RTWs from the weekday 15 allocation. Frequency reductions elsewhere saw Walworth become an RTW garage, the first ex-tram depot to do so, for the 45, 176 and 176A. Route 176 had a partial allocation of RTWs from Willesden garage on Saturdays from 1956 and this became daily in 1959. RTLs took over from both garages in 1960, as recorded in the October 1960 schedule book, but RTWs returned to Walworth in 1961 and Willesden in 1962.

New route 106A (Finsbury Park to Dagenham) was introduced with RTWs on 26th November 1958 replacing route 106 on Sundays. On the same date new route 74A was introduced with RTWs. This ran in Monday to Friday peak hours between Marylebone Station and Putney Heath, with seven journeys per day extended to Roehampton Vale. On 18th August 1963 the route was diverted from Marylebone to serve the Zoo and terminate at Camden Town.

Back to 1958, Middle Row also took over route 18B from Willesden, along with its RTWs, but this allocation was short-lived as the RTWs went off to Walworth ten months later for route 185; routes 18/18B reverting to RTL from 14th October 1959. Putney Bridge closed on 26th November 1958, with its RTWs transferring mostly to nearby Chelverton Road.

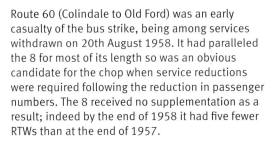

Opposite: RTW 363 sets off from Hammersmith's Riverside garage just after midnight on 21st June 1958 on the first London bus service journey to be made following the end of that year's six-week long bus strike. It repeats a scene from 21 years earlier, albeit with a different type of bus, when a crowd gathered at the same garage to watch the first bus (again on route 11) begin work after a one-month bus strike in May 1937. *Capital Transport collection*

Route 60 (Colindale to Old Ford) was an early casualty of the bus strike, being among services withdrawn on 20th August 1958. It had paralleled the 8 for most of its length so was an obvious candidate for the chop when service reductions were required following the reduction in passenger numbers. The 8 received no supplementation as a result; indeed by the end of 1958 it had five fewer RTWs than at the end of 1957.

Route 102 received weekend RTWs again in the first set of schedule revisions following the bus strike. Chingford, Royal Forest Hotel, another Central bus outpost reached by RTWs, is the setting for this view of RTW 26 in 1959.

Route 106A was introduced on 26th November 1958 to replace the 106 on Sundays, being re-routed on that day at Barking to run to Dagenham instead of Becontree. Also introduced on the same day was the 74A, running between Marylebone and the top end of Kingston Vale, where it served the growing Alton East housing estate at Roehampton. *Peter Mitchell and Ray Golds*

Routes 176 and 176A were beneficiaries of RTWs in November 1958 following service cuts on RTW routes. Walworth garage received the type for the first time and its RTW 407 is seen in Brondesbury in 1959. The 176 was shared with Willesden garage, which had been running RTWs on the route on Saturdays since 1956. Willesden also used RTWs on Mondays to Fridays within six months of the Walworth conversion and these continued with a brief absence until 1965. *Gerald Mead*

Sunday only route 23A was another casualty of the 26th November cuts, when it was withdrawn and partly replaced on its busiest section between Poplar and Aldgate by new Sunday route 95A (RT worked until 1964). RTW 59 is seen at the route's western terminus, Ladbroke Grove. *Peter Mitchell*

Route 24 first received a part-allocation of RTWs (alongside RTLs) in 1956, when 22 became available from service frequency cuts around the network. After the bus strike it was possible to make the allocation fully RTW. The route did not immediately suffer from allocation cuts resulting from the strike and eight RTWs replaced the same number of RTLs.

Route 185 was worked with RTWs on Sundays only from 26th November 1958 and part of the allocation was daily from 13th May to 11th November 1959. RTWs remained on Sundays only for another six months after that. RTW 425 is seen in Vauxhall Bridge Road. *Prince Marshall, The Bus Archive*

The Sixties

November 1959 saw RTWs go to an ex-trolleybus depot for the first time, when Clay Hall closed, the RTW allocation and routes transferring to nearby Bow. April 1960 saw some on trolleybus replacement route 123, from Tottenham garage, operating alongside Routemasters. RTWs were also involved in services that were revised as part of the conversion programme, these being the 39, 41 and 45.

Once the Routemasters had completed their first task of displacing the trolleybuses in 1962 they inevitably started to displace the RTWs from the high profile central London routes. Putney's allocation on the 14 was replaced from October 1963. RTWs took up new duties on route 95, working from Brixton, where the buses were used on Sunday-only route 57A also. November saw large-scale displacement from the 24, with the high-numbered Chalk Farm buses largely being spread around the other RTW garages, in turn displacing low-numbered examples into the training fleet all over London. Wide Leylands replaced green RTLs in the training fleet. February 1964 saw them replaced on Tottenham's 123 and 41. They also went from Upton Park's 15 and interworked 100, in April, the RTWs from these routes moving to Brixton for the 109.

In 1965 many were displaced by RTLs, and then by RMs, at Bow (8, 8A), Willesden (8, 6, 6B, 46, 176), Hackney (6, 6A), Battersea and Chalk Farm. Early in 1966 they disappeared in droves – from Chalk Farm, where the conversion to RM had started towards the end of 1965 (45, 31), Walworth (45), Hackney (106), Dalston (11), Riverside (11), Hackney (22). They then remained only at relative newcomer Brixton, where they survived until May on the 95 and 109. The last day of passenger service was 14th May 1966, with RTW 467 the final one to run in.

The 123 (Ilford to Manor House) was introduced under stage six of the trolleybus replacement programme and, working alongside fifteen Walthamstow RMs, seven RTWs were allocated to it from Tottenham. The route replaced the 41's Mon-Fri peak hour extension to Ilford, running there daily from the conversion date of 27th April 1961. RTW 53 is seen at Manor House. The offside route numbers were to disappear when an instruction went out in November 1963 to garages to cease displaying them. *Gerald Mead*

The 41, the pioneer RTW route, also played a part in the sixth stage of trolleybus replacement, when on 27th April 1960 a minority West Ham allocation was added using RMs and the route was withdrawn, except on Sundays, between Archway and Tottenham Hale. Its Mon-Fri peak extension from Tottenham Hale to Ilford being lost to the 123, the route was instead extended on Mons-Sats to Stratford Broadway via Leyton. In the meantime, after being exclusively allocated RTWs from 1949 to 1958, on 26th November 1958 a short-lived Sunday-only allocation of seven RTs from Holloway garage had been added. The 41 continued with RTWs until January 1964, making it the second longest RTW allocation, after the 74. Trafficator 'ears' were added to London's buses in 1960. *Peter Mitchell*

Route 39, which back in 1950 had been the first to penetrate the heart of central London with RTWs on a permanent basis, featured in the ninth stage of the trolleybus replacement programme, when it was extended from Camden Town to Parliament Hill Fields on 1st February 1961. *Alan B. Cross, The Bus Archive*

On the same date, route 45 also had an extension over former trolleybus routes. The route, which operated from a southern terminus at South Kensington, was doubled in length with a projection from Farringdon Street to Hampstead Heath (South End Green) to part replace trolleybuses 513/613. *Peter Mitchell*

The number 39A is the only case where a route number for two different services was used on RTWs. The first 39A had been withdrawn on 26th November 1956 after less than a year of life. The second one, a Saturday only service between Southfields and Parliament Hill Fields, was even unluckier, lasting just four and a half months from its date of introduction of 14th August 1963. It was operated with six RTWs from Battersea garage and six RTs from Holloway. Via blinds using upper and lower case lettering began to appear in the latter part of 1961. *Peter Mitchell*

A late, and fairly short lived, addition to the list of routes scheduled to be operated by RTWs was the 1, which had primarily been a New Cross operation. Between 30th January 1965 and 26th November 1965, five RTWs from Willesden were allocated on Saturdays only, after which RTLs took over the AC allocation. The introduction of the type on this day coincided with a Saturday extension to Catford along with a Monday to Friday extension to Bromley. *Michael Beamish*

Willesden garage's RTL 1338 gives a good comparison in appearance as it stands directly alongside RTW 214 in the garage yard that served also as the western terminus stand of route 8.

Route 74B was introduced late in the life of the RTW as a variation of the 74 running between Camden Town and Hammersmith. RTW 73 is seen at the Buck Street, Camden Town end of the route in August 1963, the month in which this route number was first used. RMs took over in autumn of the following year. This bus carries two versions of the BESI plate holders. *Peter Mitchell*

Route 15 continued to supply buses for Beckton Gas Works route 100 until RMs took over these services in March and April 1964. When converted to RTW back in 1951, the number of RTWs needed for the 15 was 62. By the time they left the route, the scheduled requirement had reduced to 43. RTW 54 is seen approaching the large R White's lemonade factory south of Barking Town Centre. *Capital Transport*

From 12th October 1963 route 47 received a Saturday only allocation of six RTWs from Dalston garage, running alongside RTLs from the same shed and RTs from Bromley and Catford. The RTWs also sometimes appeared on the route on Sundays, when the service was extended deep into Kent to terminate at Farnborough. RTW 116 is seen in Bishopsgate on one such working. *Alan B. Cross, The Bus Archive*

Route 34B continued to operate with RTWs off route 76 until converted to RML operation in November 1965 and this photograph was taken the previous year. *Alan B. Cross, The Bus Archive*

RTWs returned to the 85 – this time on Saturdays only – in May 1963 and remained until the route was converted to RM in August of the same year. Photographic evidence shows that the route had visits by RTWs prior to 1963. *Denis Battams*

Brixton had an allocation of RTWs for the first time on 1st October 1963, when routes 95 and 95A were converted to the type using buses released by the conversion of route 14 to RM. When route 24 followed with RMs in December the RTWs were spread around the fleet, Willesden getting the most with a total of five and three going for training duties at Muswell Hill, Hounslow and Hendon. The RM programme brought a new niche for the RTWs. Being 8ft wide they made ideal trainers for drivers who would have to manoeuvre the RMs through City and suburban streets *Denis Battams and Norman Rayfield, 2RT2 Preservation Group*

Brixton received further RTWs on 1st April 1964, this time for the 109 and the Sunday-only 57A. These were the last existing routes to receive RTWs and the scheduled allocation of RTWs to Brixton garage now totalled 58. The writing was on the wall for the RTW by now and, in the same month, examples of the type were demoted to permanent training duties. RTW 467 overtakes RTW 476 outside their home garage and RTW 15 is seen in Victoria. *Capital Transport*

The 6A was a supplementary service on the eastern end of route 6, beginning as a peak hour only route and becoming all day Mon-Sat by 1957. In February 1964, together with the new 6B, it replaced route 6 on Saturdays for a time. *Fred Ivey*

The last new route to be introduced with an allocation of RTWs was the 6B, a Saturday only route between Willesden Garage and Chingford Royal Forest Hotel (though Willesden's RTW allocation is believed to have got no further than Chingford Mount). The route was a combination of the 6 and the 257, both of which were withdrawn on that day of the week. Walthamstow provided RMs for its share of the route. The first day of operation was 1st February 1964 and RMs took over almost exclusively from 3rd April the following year. *Michael Beamish*

Route 74 was the route that had an allocation of RTWs for the longest time: October 1950 to November 1965. The 74, 74A and 74B were converted to RM on 7th November. Before then short workings between Baker Street or Marylebone to the Zoo or Camden Town were introduced from Chalk Farm garage. These were precursors of the 74X and 74Z services introduced in the 1970s. RTW 452 is seen on the stand at the Zoo end of the service. *Peter Jones*

Route 11 was converted to RM in 1966 and in February of that year RTW 413 was placed in store. No steering column gear-change is fitted to this RTW, which was transferred to Riverside garage following its third and final overhaul in early 1962. Gear-change was accomplished via a pedestal to the driver's left linked to a pneumo-cyclic gearbox. The bus was popularly known as the 'one-legger' and considered experimental by London Transport. The equipment was fitted in June 1954 to Leyland chassis number 502458, which had originally supported the body built for RTW 389. It was never removed and the same body and chassis combination later became RTW 375 and finally RTW 413. This view was taken in Fulham in August 1964. *Gerald Mead*

The last RTW to run on the last night of the type in service, 14th/15th May 1966, was RTW 467, which was bought by a group of 12 enthusiasts from London Transport on 28th February 1967 and was the first RTW to be saved for preservation. Today the bus is jointly owned by Leon Daniels OBE and Lord Hendy of Richmond Hill. Here it is seen, suitably decorated, at the Cannon Street terminus prior to its last journey. *Colin Stannard*

RTW 10 spent time as the Chiswick Works skid bus, officially allocated to nearby Turnham Green garage, between January 1967 and May 1969, playing a part in the training of new drivers. *Mick Webber*

The RTWs had their service life shortened a few years owing to pressure from the staff union. Compared with the RT and RM, drivers disliked their heavier steering, partly due to Leyland's steering mechanism – shared with the RTLs – and partly due to the heavier weight of the RTW. RTWs in particular needed their steering lubrication to be done properly to reduce the problem and not all garages did it well enough. The type – again in common with the RTL – also suffered from less smooth gear changing, something that affected the passenger experience also. Both types had the same Leyland 0.600 9.8litre engine which was less refined than the AEC 9.6litre engine fitted to RTs. Leylands always had a lumpy tickover compared to AECs. Again the extra 6cwt made them slightly more sluggish than the RTLs, and which were in turn never as sprightly as RTs.

Beginning in April 1964, many went into the training fleet and stayed there to take over from RTLs and RTs. Even Country Area garages with Routemaster types used RTWs as trainers but they all retained their red livery. 130 RTWs were maintained in the training fleet from 1966 onwards, but in 1969 the decision was made to standardise the training and staff bus fleets on RTs to alleviate the worsening spares situation. The RTW trainers started to disappear in late 1969, heading to Wombwell Diesels in Yorkshire. The Country Area trainers returned in December 1969, just before the split-off to London Country, although the Country Area used them to the last gasp: some were even allocated outwards to the country for a brief period in December. But even in the Central Area they were going, and during 1970 the last went into store, even the Chiswick skid bus, and the very last – RTW 185 – was sold in May 1971, fittingly for preservation.

Unscheduled Operations

Although for much of their lives, the RTWs were officially restricted to nominated routes, they did stray onto others – some instances being very rare. How rare can never be established as they were dependent on being recorded by enthusiasts when seen and no doubt there were operations not seen.

The earliest RTWs to be licensed for use on specific outer routes were fitted with blinds containing only the appropriate ones, rather than the normal blinds at the garages with all the routes. This was to avoid inadvertently putting an RTW out on a route not approved for them. The blinds were clearly marked with 'RTW' or 'RTW ONLY' on their ends. With the introduction on selected central London routes the practice of providing blinds stamped 'RTW' continued. To begin with these blinds only contained the routes usually scheduled for RTW operation, but with the passage of time the practice fell down. At some garages, such as Battersea, with so many of its routes run with RTWs, towards the end the 'RTW' wording was dropped and all blinds contained all its routes and were fitted to any bus. At other garages a proportion of blinds continued to be stamped 'RTW' but contained all of the garage's routes. When it came to the RTW conversion of Brixton routes it is likely that the blinds were transferred from the RTLs they replaced except where in poor condition.

How rare it was for an RTW to work on the N87 is unknown, as night routes usually went unseen except by night workers. Denis Battams managed to photograph one at Clapham South early one morning after the conversion of routes 95/95A and 109 to the type at Brixton garage.

Routes 26 and 27 saw them more often. The 26 was a trolleybus replacement route introduced in 1960 and but for delays in the production of RMs (and a coincidental surplus of RTs) would have been RM operated. RTW 154 is seen at Whitechapel and RTW 34 at Hammersmith, both photos being taken in 1964. *Gerald Mead and Alan B. Cross*

Route 30 saw RTWs fairly often, but the 37 has only one known operation recorded by this chance photograph (though there may of course have been others). The date of the 37 working with RTW 263 is not known but the painted over offside route plate holder dates it to 1964 or 1965, during which period RMs were the official allocation on the route. RTW 159 on the 30 was photographed at Roehampton. *Denis Battams, 2RT2 Preservation Group*

Routes 68 and 133 rarely saw RTWs (so far as is known), and these two views were taken during Monday to Friday evening peaks. Chalk Farm's RTW 19 is seen on the 68 at Waterloo opposite the Old Vic, and Brixton's RTW 27 is seen at Liverpool Street. *Colin Stannard* and *Capital Transport*

The 73 was one of the very first routes to be converted to RM after completion of trolleybus replacement, so 8ft wide buses (but not RTWs) were normal when this photo of RTW 345 was taken at King's Cross in June 1963. *Gerald Mead*

Putney garage's 93 route got Saturday RMs in June 1964, but before then eight-footers made occasional appearances on it in the shape of RTWs. One such working is shown at the Fulham end of Putney Bridge. *Alan B. Cross, The Bus Archive*

Route 191 first saw 8ft wide buses in February 1964, when the Saturday allocation from Tottenham garage was converted to RM. Tottenham's route 259 was RM worked from its introduction in April 1961. Both were therefore shown to be suitable for RTWs when these photos were taken. RTW 205 is seen at Hall Lane, Chingford in February 1964 and RTW 46 is seen at Edmonton on the weekend extension of the 259 to Waltham Cross, the farthest north an RTW would have ventured in LT service. *Ron Wellings* and *Alan Mortimer*

Afterlife

In late 1964, London Transport issued tender forms listing the first of the RTWs which had become surplus to requirements heralding the start of an operation that was destined to last for seven years.

The first buyer was Bird's Commercial Motors of Stratford-upon-Avon, no stranger to handling redundant LT vehicles, the company having bought and resold or scrapped many vehicles which had operated on the capital's streets including RTs, RTLs and trolleybuses. The initial batch of RTWs included RTWs 37, 110 and 117 all of which became Bird's property in February 1965. For the next few months until January 1966, the company purchased 18 of the type and found buyers for all. RTW 37 was sold immediately to the Porthcawl Omnibus Co who ran the vehicle until October 1967 when it was withdrawn after hitting a tree. Thereafter it languished at Cardiff Dock and was eventually scrapped in May 1979. RTW 117 was also swiftly sold being acquired by Kenfig Motors Ltd of Bridgend with whom it ran until June 1970. And a beat group by the name of Andy's Clappers purchased RTW 110 in March 1965, that ended its days at Harper Brothers as a spares source in September of the following year. Of the remaining fifteen vehicles acquired by Birds, four were sold to A1 Services of Ardrossan in Ayrshire and another to Red Rover of Aylesbury. RTW 178 was purchased by Stevenson's of Spath and upon withdrawal became a preservation project; it maintains Stevenson's livery. RTW 347 was acquired by St Michael's School, Ingoldisthorpe Norfolk, replacing RT 103, which the School had bought from Bird's in September 1960.

F Ridler of Whitton in Middlesex was another earlier purchaser of RTWs, the company acquiring seven of the type during 1965 all of which were

Former RTW 5 (23SRl2579) is seen near Colombo Fort on Christmas Eve 1970. The pronounced lean on this bus will be noted, caused by chronic overloading on these vehicles. *Barry Wilkinson*

Three RTW buses were exported to Double Deck Tours, Niagara Falls in 1965. Former RTW 128 (KGK 628) was acquired in June 2012 by Beth Milne and Emily Leonard and converted into the Casero Taco Bus, Sauble Beach, Ontario. It was pictured on 14 September 2017 and was still in business in 2024. *Paul Bateson*

A1 Services of Ardrossan in Scotland was another keen buyer of former London Transport buses, taking RTs, RTLs and four RTWs. RTW 184 was used by them between 1965 and the beginning of 1971.

sent for scrap to a breakers in Hertfordshire. Ridler had been quite active in purchasing other redundant LT vehicles, the majority dispatched to various breakers but these were the only RTWs acquired.

During October 1965 RTW 371 was sold to North's of Leeds; it was broken up the following March. North had attained a reputation for the buying and selling of London Transport vehicles but only secured sixteen RTWs; three in 1966 and twelve in 1968; six of the company's purchases were sold to other operators, the rest were scrapped.

The latter months of 1965, saw the commencement of the despatch of RTWs to Ceylon, the country having become a significant destination for the Board's surplus RT family vehicles. Eventually 279 of the type were shipped to the Ceylon Transport Board of Colombo, most departing England during 1966 and the remainder in 1967.

As the sixties drew to a close, two companies became involved with the scrapping of the RTWs. Wombwell Diesels, to the south of Barnsley, was responsible for the demise of 35, the first, RTW 373, being acquired in October 1965 when the company was known as Hoyles. Four years were to elapse before the next five vehicles were purchased by Wombwell Diesels: RTW 25 and RTW 482 in April 1969 and RTW 254, 313 and RTW 430 in May. In November and December of the same year and January of 1970 24 RTWs also achieved one way tickets to Wombwell apart from RTW 29 which became the subject of a preservation project soon returning south and after passing through the hands of four preservationists, it is now in the safekeeping of JJP Holdings South West Ltd. Also included among this batch was RTW 100,

Barton Transport of Chilwell operated a well-presented variety of buses. Pictured in Ilkeston on 1st September 1967 is fleet number 1035 which was formerly RTW 341. *Paul Bateson*

Red Rover, Aylesbury was well known for operating a number of former London Transport double deckers. The former RTW 124 became fleet number RR5 in its fleet and is seen in Aylesbury on 1st July 1968. *Paul Bateson*

which had been involved in an an experiment within the confines of Stonebridge garage. As the vehicle had been identified for scrap following an accident, opportunity was taken to test the effect of continuous running of a fluid flywheel at maximum stalled speed; the bus subsequently burst into flames after an explosion.

However, Wombwell Diesels' association with the destruction of the RTW class was surpassed by the involvement of Pickersgill & Laverick, whose scrapyard was at Cudworth, north of Barnsley. In acquiring 110 vehicles, among them RTW 1, the company and Wombwell Diesels disposed of approximately 30% of the fleet.

The fates of some of the remaining 75 RTWs that did not immediately head north for scrapping or find a new home in Ceylon have already been mentioned. A further ten were exported, the largest group comprising RTW 96, RTW 161, RTW 175 and RTW 186 were shipped to South Africa where they entered service with the City Tramways Co of Cape Town in the summer of 1965. RTW 127, RTW 128 and RTW 148 were purchased by N Watson of Chippea, Ontario, whose company Doubledeck Tours used the buses to transport tourists to the Niagara Falls. The vehicles retained their LT livery after repainting and all later saw service as food outlets.

Of the remaining three RTWs to leave the UK, RTW 417 was sent to the Netherlands to become a mobile showroom for Carnaby Street clothes in June 1969. Unfortunately the clearances on some overbridges in this country, despite being of 20th Century construction, preclude the passage beneath of double deck buses and it is little wonder that the vehicle ended up in a scrapyard with roof damage just a year later.

Two RTWs went to West Germany; RTW 157 was purchased by H A Turner of Hanover

Mason's Coaches of Darlaston bought RTW 187 from Bird's Commercial Motors in July 1966 and ran it until December 1970.

RTW 489 saw brief use as a mobile furniture showroom for a company in Nazeing between March 1966 and May 1967, then passing through two dealers before ending up with another furniture company, this time in Wigan.

and was used to promote Burberry and other British fashion houses. RTW 335 was acquired by J Schwalen and used as a hospitality bus for vehicle lifts produced by Hywema. It was eventually returned to the UK and left with an operator for restoration. The vehicle then passed to Ensignbus who engaged Bus Works of Blackpool to undertake its restoration. RTW 335 is now active as part of the fleet of preserved vehicles owned by Heritage Vehicle Management Ltd (Newman Family).

Other dealers purchased RTWs from London Transport for resale. Arlington Motors of Potters Bar secured two examples: RTW 151 and RTW 329 in December 1965 and January 1966. After passing through the ownership of four operators RTW 151 became a a preservation project in December 1979. RTW 329 became staff transport for the clothing company Gor-Ray and upon withdrawal from these duties also became a preserved vehicle in November 1975; both have yet to make their debut in restored condition.

Passenger Vehicle Sales of Upminster purchased six RTWs between February and June 1966. All were sold by PVS to other operators: RTW 256 to Osborne's of Tollesbury, RTW 301 to Broadway Coaches of Wickford, RTW 413, retaining its pneumocyclic gearbox, to Super Coaches of Upminster later becoming part of the Lesney contract fleet and RTW 429 to OK Motor Services. RTW 429 was initially preserved in OK Motor Services livery but its longevity in this capacity failed and it was scrapped in 1980. PVS also sold RTW 456 to Buckmasters of Leighton Buzzard together with its last purchase of the type, RTW 497 which eventually became a preservation project, passing through the ownership of three individuals before being acquired by Tony Potter who completed the restoration.

RTW 151 was used for private hire work by three separate companies between December 1965 and 1971. After passing through two dealers it was then bought for preservation by Roger Wright, who still owns it. This view shows it with Denham Coaches of Iver Heath.

Other RTWs were purchased directly from London Transport for preservation: RTW 467 was purchased by a group of 12 in March 1971 and two months later Fraser Clayton purchased RTW 185 – the last of the type to leave LT's ownership. Ted Brakell's first purchase of an LT vehicle was RT 44 from a scrapyard for use as a store for his company's decorating materials. However, he soon changed his mind and decided that it should enter the ranks of preserved vehicles. Ted was later offered RTW 75 by LT which came into his possession on 23 January 1970; it is now the property of the London Bus Company.

Some operators successfully tendered for vehicles as they became available, notably Cresta Coaches of London SW9 (RTW 284 and RTW 387), Margo's Coaches of Penge, (RTW 176, which later became a racing car transporter and RTW 195), Viola Coaches of London SE22 (RTW 26), Roydonian Coaches of Roydon, Essex (RTW 367) and Barton Transport of Chilwell, Nottinghamshire (RTW 341). Three companies purchased vehicles for staff bus use: Trollope and Colls (RTW 87), Agent Engineering of Dartford (RTW 304) and Ford and Walton (RTW 130) whilst others required them for showrooms: Decca (RTW 208) and the Wrighton Aircraft Company (RTW 489).

In October 1970, T Collins of Stepney successfully tendered for the remains of RTW 84 which had been severely damaged in a garage fire at Poplar.

Occasionally a preserved RTW has made an appearance on television or in a feature film. Perhaps the most memorable for a certain generation was the arrival at a suburban house of RTW 75 in an episode of *Monty Python's Flying Circus* to pick up three members of the 'Spanish Inquisition'.

RTW 413 was purchased by Passenger Vehicle Sales in April 1966 whereupon it became the property of Super Coaches of Upminster. A paper transfer in November 1968 saw the vehicle being operated by Upminster and District whose fleetname appears on the vehicle in this view. PVS and the Upminster operations were closely linked and in January 1969 the bus could be found on contract to Lesney Products in Hackney as a staff bus. No further details were received regarding the vehicle following its acquisition by Barraclough a dealer, at Rosyton, Yorkshire. The gear change column fitted to the vehicle was similar to that shown below right.

Viola Coaches of East Dulwich was one of the operators that purchased RTWs directly from London Transport. This is RTW 26, the sale to Viola recorded as 1st June 1966. *Norman Rayfield, 2RT2 Bus Preservation Group*

Cresta Coaches of SW19 purchased two RTWs from London Transport at different times: RTW 284 was acquired on 9th September 1965 and RTW 387 on 10th February 1966. Both were pressed into service on 1st July 1977 when they were hired by local Scout groups to provide transport to that year's rally held at Gilwell Park, Chingford; RTW 284 is seen leaving the site. Both vehicles were sold to Fisher & Ford, a dealer in Barnsley, in March 1969. *Norman Rayfield, 2RT2 Bus Preservation Group*

Some RTWs were sold directly by London Transport for preservation whilst others saw service with other organisations before achieving this status. RTW 497 is one such example having been acquired by Passenger Vehicle Sales of Upminster in June 1966 and being moved in the same month to Buckmaster Coaches of Leighton Buzzard. After its sale to a local dealer in July 1971, the vehicle was purchased for preservation being owned separately by three individuals, the last being Tony Potter of Edgware in whose possession it has been since October 1979. The vehicle is seen at County Hall on 23rd May 1971. *Norman Rayfield, 2RT2 Bus Preservation Group*

An example of the class sold for staff transport is RTW 130 seen here in an east London street two months after its direct sale to Ford & Walton of Stratford, E15 on 28th February 1966. *Norman Rayfield, 2RT2 Bus Preservation Group*

An Example of Preservation

RTW 185 was completed at Leyland on 29th November 1949 and was received at Chiswick Works on 9th December 1949. With RTWs 180–184 and 186–189 it went to Putney Bridge garage on 14th December 1949 for Route 85. It was used, on loan to other garages, in all three of the 1950 width trials.

RTW 185's first overhaul was in September 1953 at Aldenham after which it returned to Putney Bridge for route 14 or route 74 until its next overhaul in June 1957, following which it was allocated to Willesden on routes 6 and 8, staying there until its last overhaul in April 1961. Its last service garage was Bow on route 8, following which it became a trainer. So, as it had been in the very beginning, RTW 185 became a training vehicle once again. It was used and delicensed, then used again several times. Garages allocated were Holloway and Muswell Hill until finally delicensed at Clapton on 13th June 1970.

Without going into the finer details here, the overhaul process at Aldenham was noteworthy in that the original RTW 185 chassis and body remained together for all its life, the pair becoming RTW 246 in July 1957 and RTW 211 in March 1961. That RTW 185 was one of the large number of the type sold to Ceylon/Sri Lanka.

The present RTW 185 began life as RTW 183. The chassis became RTW 222 in April 1957 and then RTW 185 in March 1961. The body was on RTW 163 in April 1957 and then RTW 185 in March 1961. It is therefore remarkable that the present body and chassis started life together in 1949 and came together again at the last overhaul in 1961, and is now only two numbers away from original RTW 183 – RTW 185. However, as it has been known as RTW 185 for 63 years to date, it will keep that identity.

RTW 185 at the Alton Bus Rally in July 2022. *Matthew Jimmison*

During its LT life it had a Certificate of Fitness in 1949 for five years, then in November 1953 for five years, and in June 1957 and April 1961 for seven years each.

Owner Fraser Clayton writes:

I purchased RTW 185 in May 1971 direct from LT at which time it was languishing at the back of Clapton garage between two other RTWs which subsequently went for scrap, and it was the last Leyland of the RT family to be owned by LT. When collecting RTW 185 from Clapton Garage, once the foreman realised it was going into preservation and not for scrap, he could not have been more helpful. Whilst owned by LT and then by myself it has been on the road every year since manufacture in 1949.

As I have been involved in fleet maintenance as my career, the mechanical and body condition of RTW 185 has always been kept up to standard and it could go back into service again tomorrow. A great deal of restoration work has been carried out by myself on this double decker over the years, and all the minor modifications made during its LT working life have been put back to as-delivered condition, all carried out by myself including paintwork. These mods were fairly superficial items – no mechanical alterations or major body surgery were needed.

The Leyland chassis and body were of a good quality and therefore worked well. However we must acknowledge that the steering was heavier than an RT, although changing the front wheels to standard RT ones did not help as the originals had more offset. Complaints about poor engine tickover and 'hunting' are unfounded as a simple adjustment to the injection pump and idle screw makes them tickover like a clock. After acquisition by me, the modifications required to put RTW 185 back to original condition were:

- cream upper deck window surrounds in place of red
- masking of blind boxes for austerity blind layout
- dumb iron covers (reinstated length)
- radiator blinds (reinstated)
- direction indicators on the front ('ears') removed (indicators now hidden)
- front wheel nut guards back to Leyland aluminium ones (not RT steel ones)
- riveted wheels have been fitted (correct offsets on fronts)
- one piece rear lower panel replaced around number plate
- reflectors removed (now a temporary fitting)
- rear upper deck emergency window guttering replaced (was altered to look like an RT)
- nearside mirror arm put back to upside down 'U' shape (not straight)
- battery booster socket under the driver's foothold reinstated
- beading around the rear mudguards painted red (not black)
- 3/8" cream line around the Route Number box over the bonnet reinstated
- original headlamps and spot lamp reinstated
- extra guardrail on luggage area on platform removed
- offside rear lower corner panel replaced (metal not rubber)
- aperture at the top of the stairs, for cleaning purposes, has been removed
- green Rexine covered horizontal beading re-installed between the lower green interior window surrounds and the brown Rexine below.

All of this has made the vehicle as near as possible to original 1949 specification. In addition to the above work of mine, some seats were reupholstered by a professional upholsterer and sets of restricted destination blinds were produced at Aldenham.

Since my ownership from 1971 RTW 185 has attended countless rallies and road runs, displays etc all over the country and abroad. In fact in 1972 it was invited to participate in an event involving a contingent of vintage vehicles going over to France and on to Turin, Italy, travelling a total of 1700 miles over 3 weeks including going over the Alps at 7110 feet!

In 1993 it ventured to the Isle of Man for its Transport Festival (also attended by Fred Dibnah) crossing on a freight ferry from Heysham to Douglas on a flat calm Irish Sea each way. The bus has also attended many HCVS London to Brighton Runs, Plymouth Bus Rally, HCVS Trans Pennine Run, Great Dorset Steam Fair and Isle of Wight events. It has also appeared at numerous Leyland and London Transport events including Leyland 100 at Leyland in 1996, RT50 celebrations in Covent Garden, RTW50 rally at Cobham Bus Museum in 1999 (organised by my good friend the late Roy Adams) and RTW60 at Alton Bus Rally in 2009, plus various LT garage open days including the events held at Chiswick and Aldenham, also RT75 at Ash Grove garage in April 2014.

RTW 185 has been fortunate in that for the first four years in my ownership it lived in the summer in a secure yard in Belmont, Surrey, and in winter tucked up in a WW2 hangar at Eastleigh Airport (Southampton). It then gained its own garage with one or two other vehicles at my home.

APPENDIX 1:
RTW REGISTRATION NUMBERS

1-150	KGK501-650
151-250	KLB881-980
251-350	KXW351-450
351-450	LLU501-600
451-500	LLU941-990

APPENDIX 2:
RTWs PRESERVED

RTW 29: active preservation, UK, by JJP Holdings South West Ltd
RTW 75: actively preserved by Blue Triangle
RTW 151: in UK
RTW 178: preserved with doors, rear emergency door and yellow Stevensons livery.
RTW 185: active preservation, UK
RTW 329: in UK
RTW 335: active preservation, UK. Now part of the Heritage Vehicle Management Fleet (Newman Family) having been returned to the UK after spending time in France and Germany.
RTW 467: active preservation, UK
RTW 497: active preservation, UK

APPENDIX 3, supplied by Lawrie Bowles:
RTW OVERHAULING

Overhauling of RTWs started with RTW 1, which went to works on 31st October 1951. The process was to separate body from chassis and send the latter to Chiswick for repair. The bodies were referred to by their own numbers, RTW 1-500: 2901-3400, but the chassis was allocated a serial number in the order they were booked in, which in almost all cases was the actual order. The series was 6001-6500, which followed the RT series, so RTW 1's chassis was allocated 6001. After work, the chassis and body were reunited and it came out as RTW 1 on 27th November. RTW 2 was next in, on 6th January 1952 and out on 18th, and other pre-series overhauls were RTW 6, in on 25th April, RTW 46 on 13th May, RTW 29 on 18th August, RTW 27 on 27th and RTW 7 on 18th November, these allocated 6002-7. Series overhauling then started in January 1953 with RTWs 12, 5, 69, and then speeding up from February. Overhaul intakes continued until 17th November 1954. In all cases, the same body emerged on the chassis it had gone in on.

By the time the second cycle was due, the Works Float system was in full operation at Aldenham. Again, a few were dealt with early as one-offs, beginning with RTW 1 from 1st September 1955 to 19th October and RTW 2 from 23rd September to 1st November. The series proper started when the next 21 buses were taken on to what was known as the Works Float, where the bus was delicensed with no replacement going on the road immediately. These numbers were 4, 5, 7, 9, 11, 12, 13, 14, 15, 16, 19, 21, 22, 23, 25, 32, 33, 35, 68, 69 and 74.

These fleet numbers disappeared until completion of the cycle in 1958, except for RTWs 69 and 74 which re-emerged in June 1957 when the float was reduced. Most bodies were reunited with their original chassis, but now carrying different fleet numbers. A small number of chassis/body combinations were altered during the series. After completion of it, the Works Float was disbanded. RTWs 220/27/35/39/40/42 gained the bodies from RTWs 235/20/39/42/27/40 respectively, RTWs 244/46 exchanged bodies, as did RTWs 261/68, RTWs 267/75, RTWs 272/80, RTWs 339/43, RTWs 366/73. RTWs 374/75/85/87 gained bodies 3285/87/74/5 respectively, RTWs 436/37 swapped bodies as did RTWs 442/45.

The third and final cycle of overhauls became due in 1959-60. The only early overhaul this series was RTW 17, in 2nd November 1959 to 29th December. Nineteen vehicles were then taken on to the Works Float: RTWs 1, 2, 3, 6, 8, 18, 20 26, 27, 29, 36, 38, 52, 59, 63, 65, 67 and 90. All these remained as float until March 1962.

After those RTW 55 went in on 29th August, nominally to the float, but it emerged on 17th September to Willesden (AC), this being the original RTW 1, body and chassis. RTW71 went in for overhaul on 31st August and RTW 58 on 1st September, as the first two regular overhauls of the final series, followed by RTWs 24 and 84.

Series overhauls finished in March 1962, and the float was then dispersed as follows: 6th March RTW 38. 9th RTW 1. 12th: RTWs 6, 65. 13th RTWs 2, 3. 16th RTW 18. 20th RTW 65. 21st RTW 26. 27th RTW 29. 28th RTW 28. 30th RTW 20. The remaining ones were formed up at the end of March but not released until 2nd April RTW 8. 3rd RTW 36. 6th RTWs 59, 63, 67, 90. Body/chassis swaps were more common during this series. This system meant that the low numbered RTWs ended up mostly with the newest bodies.